Living Beautifully

Practical Proverbs for Women

Living Beautifully

Practical Proverbs for Women

Dara Halydier

ISBN: 0985123990
ISBN 13: 9780985123994

Endorsements

"Rarely have I come across a resource as helpful as Practical Proverbs for Women. Dara Halydier clearly communicates timeless, godly principles in a pragmatic manner. She is an able guide and her teachings should inspire transformative changes!" - Dr. Les Carter, author of *The Anger Trap.*

"You'll hunger for more! Dara's teaching is saturated with Scripture – intense, imaginative and definitive. Her life is a catalyst for victorious living." – Hope Winslow, Bible teacher.

"Dara is gifted in teaching and being able to captivate an audience as a speaker. Her knowledge and love of the Word runs deep. You will surely walk away blessed and with a desire to seek a more intimate relationship with her Jesus." – Leigh O'Malley, Bible teacher

"Dara is refreshing to listen to. She is able to provide that needed roadmap of today's life with Biblical meaning. I have had the pleasure of hearing Dara speak and lead ladies of faith in different venues, and I am always pleasantly surprised by the depth of knowledge and practicality she brings to the table." – Tonya, convention coordinator

"Dara is passionate and has a true heart for teaching. She has been a wonderful mentor for me to learn from. Her wisdom is immense and she has a heart for God." – Amy, mentoring client

Other Books by Dara Halydier:

Practical Proverbs for Younger Students (Ages 8-14)
Practical Proverbs for Older Students (Ages 15-young adult)
Wisdom, Work, and Wealth (12-week Bible study for 5th grade through adult)
As They Sit and Stand: a Resource and Guide for Teaching Your Child the Bible

You can see these books at www.abidingtruthministry.com

Dedication

I dedicate this book to my wonderful husband who has encouraged me, taken me out to dinner numerous times so I could keep writing, pushed me when I wanted to quit, and has always shown the unconditional love of Jesus to me through his words and actions.

Practical Proverbs for Women: Living Beautifully Book 1

The peacock is a symbol of integrity and the beauty that we can achieve when we endeavor to show our true colors. The ancient Greeks believed that the peafowl flesh did not decay after death, so it became a symbol for the early Christian Church of immortality or eternal life. That life begins at the moment of salvation. Practical Proverbs will help you as you grow to become a woman of integrity and beauty.

Practical Proverbs is a two book Bible study course for adults with an emphasis on life management skills. Book 1 (8 weeks) covers Proverbs 1-9 systematically, and Book 2 (8 weeks) covers Proverbs 10-31 topically. They can be done as a group or independently.

Practical Proverbs for Women: Living Beautifully will look at the book of Proverbs found in the Bible: its history, its author, its intended audience. You will define some words so we are talking about the same things, and you will fill out a chart contrasting wisdom and foolishness as you cover Proverbs chapters 1-9. Topics include whole-heartedness, purpose of rules, biblical foolishness, biblical wisdom, trusting God, world views, guarding your heart, and others.

Practical Proverbs for Women: Living Gracefully, also 8 weeks, will help you to apply what you have learned as you walk through Proverbs 10-31 topically. You will learn about topics relevant to your life today such as money, anger, emotions, words, and work. Being able to file away God's wisdom, proverb by proverb, will lead you into a victorious and rich life in Christ Jesus.

Each student will do five lessons per week individually and then get together for a leader to go over discussion questions once a week. Leader's guide is at the back of the book with the answers for the blanks and discussion questions.

Unless otherwise mentioned, the Bible verses are taken from the New American Standard Bible.

God's Word is eternal and thus, foundational for every person. May God bless the study of His Word and bring you long life and wisdom and joy.

Introduction

What is wisdom? There is the wisdom of the ages, biblical wisdom, wise sayings, wise-cracks, and wise guys. Where do you find true wisdom? Is there a universal, absolute wisdom? Is wisdom knowledge, understanding, application, or maybe all three?

Wisdom has to do with choices—on what to base your choices, understanding the consequences of your choices, weighing your choices. Choices about life, relationships, money, religion, duties, and even what to wear or eat and when, with whom, and how long are addressed by the wisest man who ever lived.

Proverbs is a great place to start your treasure hunt as you search for nuggets of wisdom. Along the way you will learn about yourself, your friends, your families, and your God.

To understand wisdom, you must also look at its opposite: foolishness. What are the characteristics and results of foolish choices and of wise choices? Do my choices impact only the immediate? Could a bad choice haunt me for a very long time?

My prayer for you is that you will gain not only knowledge about wisdom, but wisdom on how to apply knowledge to your life and that you may desire God's choices for each decision you will face in your future. May you grow closer to God who delights in you and has a plan and a purpose for your life.

Practical Proverbs for Women: Living Beautifully

Week 1 / Day 1

Wisdom, Knowledge, Instruction

The proverbs of Solomon the son of David, king of Israel:
To know wisdom and instruction.
To receive instruction in wise behavior,
Righteousness, justice and equity.

PROVERBS 1:1-2, 3

My sister was just five years old and headed off to kindergarten in the 1960's. She heard talk of being bussed to another school because of the desegregation laws. In her young mind, *bussed* meant *bust—* which happens when you do something bad and the police put you in jail. With much fear and trembling she was forced onto the school bus knowing she would never see her parents again and would be put into jail. The bus pulled up to a long one story brick institution. She warily got into line. When she saw big guns were being used on each child in line (inoculations or vaccinations), she had a major breakdown. Once the teacher took her inside, settled her down and understood her fears, she was able to console and comfort a very distraught little girl.

Any word has the capacity to bring to your mind a lot of different images based upon your own experiences or interactions with the subject. To a Christian the word "God" should bring praise and anticipation, but to those who practice other religions, *god* is to be feared (literal trembling fear) and appeased.

When you hear the word *God* what is the image you see or words you think?

_____

_____

When I refer to God, I mean the God of the Bible, the Great Creator, Savior Redeemer, and Spirit of Truth. Christians *fear* our God as we recognize His authority and holiness in awe and wonder and reverence. We have no need to fear His condemnation or judgment.

Specific definitions for several words found in the book of Proverbs will clarify your study. The first word is *wisdom*. When you think of wisdom do you think of King Solomon justly judging between the two women who brought a baby before him asking him to decide which woman was the real mother (1 Kings 3:16-28)? Do you think of your dad or grandfather who taught you about life? Maybe a teacher took time and interest in you, and you think he/she had a lot of wisdom. Can wisdom be attained or is it something you are born with and can be scored like your IQ?

Write what reminds you of wisdom. _____

_____

The American Heritage Dictionary of the English Language defines wisdom as "Understanding of what is true, right, or lasting." And, "Common sense; good judgment."[1]

What in your life is true? _____

What in your life is right? _____

What in your life is lasting? _____

As Christians, we go one step deeper and define wisdom as, "Understanding what is true, right, or lasting according to God and His Word, the Bible," and, "Using biblical truths as the basis for good judgment."

Your working definition of wisdom will be: The ability to judge correctly and use our knowledge to avoid trouble, solve problems, reach goals, and succeed in life based upon God's principles.

Mark the following which would be defined as wisdom.

_____1. Learning the names of the constellations
_____2. Knowing lying is wrong and choosing to be truthful
_____3. Knowing what is for dinner
_____4. Saying no to watching inappropriate movies or television shows
_____5. Finding joy in spending time with God

Hopefully you marked numbers 2, 4, and 5.

The next word is *knowledge*. You can tell from the above exercise knowing is not the same as wisdom. Knowledge is having the facts. You should know the facts before you make a judgment or choice, but knowing is just the first step towards wisdom. If wisdom is based on making choices based on God's Word, you had better learn what God's Word says! Once you know what God would have you to do, or how He would have you respond, then you can apply wisdom.

Proverbs was written by King Solomon so his son would know wisdom and instruction. Proverbs 4:13 says, "Take hold of instruction; let her not go. Guard her, for she is your life." Instruction is knowledge gained from someone who is more knowledgeable. Instruction is putting information in order; preparing, teaching, arranging, and building up information so it can be utilized. Again, instruction, like knowledge is a precursor of wisdom. Instruction is gained by taking the Word of God and learning how it can be applied; by knowing how others have used God's words and principles and how God honored obedience in their lives.

To have wisdom, you need to first know the facts and then you need instruction—how to apply it. I used to think if I told my children the facts I could expect them to act wisely. I realized they needed an extended amount of time of instruction before they would be able to act wisely. Wisdom is evident when you take what you know and apply it to your situation, your problem, your goals, and your life.

Go back through today's lesson and write a definition for each of these words.

Wisdom:

Knowledge:

Instruction:

Begin memorizing the working definition of wisdom: The ability to judge correctly and use your knowledge to avoid trouble, solve problems, reach goals, and succeed in life based upon God's principles.

Questions to think about:

1. What is the difference between wisdom and knowledge?

2. Are you making wise decisions at work? In friendships? In family relationships?

3. How is your working definition of wisdom different than the world's view of wisdom? (See 1 Corinthians 1:18 -2:16.)

4. What knowledge is biblical wisdom based on?

5. Are you spending time studying the Bible to gain knowledge of God?

6. Begin memorizing the working definition of wisdom: "Wisdom is the ability to judge correctly and use your knowledge to avoid trouble, solve problems, reach goals, and succeed in life based upon God's principles."

Discernment, Prudence, Discretion

To discern the saying of understanding …
To give prudence to the naïve,
To the youth knowledge and discretion.

PROVERBS *1:2, 4*

My son was six-years old when we moved to a new town. He was excited to be going to Vacation Bible school. As we entered the sanctuary, I could see he was becoming very quiet and had slowed his excited run to a crawl. Tears began to form in his eyes. I took him back outside and asked him what was wrong. He couldn't tell me, but I suspected his fear had to do with new people, the new building, and not knowing what to expect. I took him by the hand we began to explore. I showed him his room, the craft room, the cafeteria, the restroom, and the gym. Then I took him back into the sanctuary and introduced him to his teacher who introduced him to a young boy his age. He looked up to me with a smile and declared, "I'm ready now. Bye, Mom."

My son had needed some facts, some information to make him feel safe. He needed some instruction on how his time at VBS would go. Only then was he able to act with wisdom and see he was safe and would have a good time.

Knowing is the facts.
Instruction is the learning about the facts and their use.
Wisdom is applying the facts by making right choices.

Proverbs was written to Solomon's son that he might, "Discern the sayings of understanding" (Prov. 1:2). What is discernment? Discernment is being able to distinguish between good and evil, leading you to act with wisdom.

If you are to act wisely, you had better know what is right, true, and lasting. There are several types of discernment. Where someone might be good at discerning people, someone else might be better at discerning current situations, and someone else might be good at discerning future plans and ideas. My husband has a keen ability to know if someone is telling the truth and working with integrity. One of my sons is very good at discerning God's will in his life for each decision, and another son is great with discerning whether a particular plan will be the best or if another ought to be considered. I excel in spiritual discernment—being able to tell if someone is a Christian or worshipping other spirits.

Discernment can be developed. Hebrews 5:14 says, "Solid food is for the mature, who because of practice have their senses trained to discern good and evil." Solid food is referring to deeper understanding and application of God's Word. Discernment is like a muscle, the more you use it the stronger it becomes. Once again, however, we find discernment is based on knowledge—knowledge of God's Word. You need to be reading the Bible. Throughout this course, you will be encouraged to develop a stronger prayer life and to be in the Word more and more.

Remember knowledge and instruction comes first followed by discernment and wisdom.
Are you discerning? Yes or No? _____

In what areas do you practice discernment? _____
_____

The next word is *prudence*. Another reason for the writing of Proverbs is "To give prudence to the naïve" (Prov. 1:4). *The American Heritage Dictionary of the English Language* defines prudent as "wise in handling practical matters, careful about one's conduct."[2] Often someone who dresses with modesty or has strict rules about where he/she can go and what he/she can do is called a prude. This is the same root word used here. The prude is careful about his conduct. To those around him who have looser rules and who don't understand God's standards, he is a prude, but to God he is being prudent.

Would your friends consider you a prude? Yes or No? _____

If you answered no, is it because your friends have the same biblical lifestyle you have or is it because your life does not measure up to biblical standards? _____
_____

Who are the naïve in Proverbs 1:4? One who is naïve has no knowledge, or having received knowledge has refused to apply it to his own life with wisdom. Do you know someone who is naïve? Are you naïve in some areas? Naivety can be used as a put down or can just be a fact. I am very naïve when it comes to understanding the mechanical workings of a car. I don't know. I don't want to know. I just put gas in it, and the car runs. This does not get me into trouble because my husband understands cars and keeps me out of trouble. On the other hand, if something was to happen to my husband, and I had to take responsibility for my car, then it could be very costly to remain naïve. I would need to seek knowledge and instruction on the care of the automobile.

At other times naivety is not acceptable. Remaining naïve about personal cleanliness, social graces, acceptable language, and most importantly, God's design for your life will get you in trouble. God is the author of creation. As the creature, you should go to Him to find out the rules of your existence. He holds the playbook, the manual, and even the end of the story in His hands.

"Proverbs can give prudence to the naïve" (Prov. 1:4). Proverbs can teach you what you don't know—what you should know. I wouldn't want to go to war without going through boot camp where I can learn how to shoot and strategize to come home alive. Proverbs is a Christian boot camp. In it is the wisdom of the Lord God your Maker. Within its words are life and success and victory and eternal life.

What are you naïve about? Does your naivety cause problems? _____

_____

_____

Just one more word to define for now—*Discretion*. Discretion is thinking about and applying wisdom before thoughts come out in words or actions. In other words, think before you speak and sometimes think and don't speak. Apply wisdom to your own life, live it out, and others will be open to hearing what you have to say. Discretion means knowing when to speak and when to be silent.

Go back through today's lesson and write a definition for each of these words.

Discernment:

Prudence:

Naïve:

Discretion:

Questions to think about:

1. How does discernment relate to wisdom?

2. Are you maturing in discernment?

3. What type of discernment are you good at applying?

4. Are you prudent in areas of modesty? Speech? Dress?

5. We tell our kids, "Just because a is in your mind, doesn't mean it needs to come out of your mouth." Is this a problem for you?

6. In what situation might you need prudence?

7. In what situation might you need discernment?

8. In what situation might you need discretion?

9. Work on memorizing the working definition of wisdom.

> "Wisdom is the ability to _____ correctly and use your _____ to avoid trouble, solve problems, reach goals, and succeed in life based upon _____ principles."

Pop Quiz

A wise man will hear and increase in learning,
And a man of understanding will acquire wise counsel.

PROVERBS 1:5

Time for a pop quiz. Try taking this quiz without looking back, then if you need to look back for a few clues go ahead. There won't be a grade.

1. Proverbs was written by
    a. King David
    b. King Solomon
    c. Jesus
    d. Confucius

2. Wisdom is the ability to judge correctly and use your knowledge to avoid trouble, solve problems, reach goals, and succeed in life based upon _____ principles.

3. According to the above definition what must be acquired before wisdom can be obtained?
    a. Experience
    b. Age
    c. Love
    d. Knowledge

4. How do you get knowledge about God's wisdom?
    a. Pray
    b. Read the Bible

    c. Listen to good Bible teachers

    d. Memorize Scripture

    e. All of the above

5. Instruction is gained by taking the _____ and learning how it can be applied; knowing how others have used God's words and principles, and how God honored their obedience and faithfulness in their lives.

6. True or False? There is only one type of discernment. _____

7. True or False? Discernment is a gift you either have or don't have; it can't be gained. _____

8. How can you get discernment?
    a. It's a gift.
    b. You have to exercise it.
    c. Only old people can get it.

9. True or False? You should make fun of someone who is a "prude." _____

10. True or False? You should have prudence and, thus, you should be a prude _____

11. True or False? Sometimes it's okay to be naïve. _____

12. It's okay to be naïve about:
    a. God's Words
    b. Automobile engines
    c. God's plan for you
    d. Wisdom

13. True or False? Discretion says if I know the answer I should always belt it right out. _____

How did you do? Are you a little wiser or do you just know more? _____

Maybe you are not as naïve and, perhaps, you are a little more discerning.

Questions to think about:

1. Explain how the fear of the Lord is the beginning of wisdom. Relate this verse to your own life.

2. Are you daily seeking to gain wisdom? How?

3. Who in your life is an example of a wise person?

4. Work on memorizing the working definition of wisdom.

    "Wisdom is the ability to _____correctly and use your _____ to avoid _____, solve problems, reach_____, and succeed in life based upon _____."

5. Begin memorizing Proverbs 1:7.

6. Read Proverbs 1:1-7 and fill in the blanks.

    The proverbs of Solomon, the son of David, king of Israel:
    To know _____ and _____,
    To _____ the sayings of _____,
    To receive _____ in wise behavior,
    Righteousness, justice and equity;
    To give _____ to the _____,
    To the youth _____ and _____,
    A wise man will hear and increase in learning,
    And a man of _____ will acquire wise counsel,
    To understand a proverb and a figure,
    The words of the wise and their riddles.
    The fear of the Lord is the beginning of _____;
    Fools despise _____ and _____.

Week 1 / Day 4

Davids Choices

The proverbs of Solomon the son of David ...
Son of Jesse ... who is a skillful musician,
a mighty man of valor, A warrior, one prudent
in speech, and a handsome man; and the Lord is with him.

PROVERBS 1:1, 1 SAMUEL 16:18

Solomon, the author of Proverbs, got his wisdom from God. You will read more about him in the next couple of days. But Solomon's dad, King David, also learned wisdom from God and through his own experiences. Today's lesson will focus on David and the most important lessons of consequences, repentance, and choices.

For this lesson you will need: a small piece of wood, 2-3 nails (any size), and a hammer.

God had established Israel in the land of Canaan. God ruled the people through judges and prophets He appointed, but the people wanted a king. Read 1 Samuel 8:7-9.

In 1 Samuel 8:7-9, whom had Israel rejected: God or Samuel? _____

In 1 Samuel 8:7-9, what was Israel's great sin? _____

_____

God reluctantly consented and had His prophet Samuel anoint Saul as king. Saul reigned 32 years over Israel, but he sinned before the Lord. God sent Samuel to tell him a prophecy of what was to come. Read 1 Samuel 13:14. This prophecy was fulfilled in David.

What characteristic would the new king have? _____

David was just a shepherd boy when Samuel anointed him king. Read 1Samuel 16:7, 12-13. Man looks at the outer appearance of men, but what does God look at? _____

When David was anointed king, what came upon him mightily? _____

Before David took the throne as king, however, he first became a musician in the king's court soothing Saul's moods and evil spirit. Read 1 Samuel 16:17-19, 23.

List the six attributes used to describe David.

David also became the king's armor bearer, the victor over Goliath, a strong warrior, the king's son's best friend, and the king's son-in-law. He was chased by the king, hunted down by the king's men and given opportunity to kill the king. David denied himself because he recognized the king was God's anointed. God watched over David through these years of treachery, betrayal, and battles. After Saul was slain and David was finally made king, God made a covenant with him through Nathan the prophet. Read 2 Samuel 7:8-17. To what does God attribute David's success? _____

_____

Who is prophesied of in 2 Samuel 7: 12, 13, 16? _____

David responded with praise and humility. Read 2 Samuel 7:18-29. Whom did David ask God to magnify? _____

David, however, soon fell to temptation and committed adultery and murder. God again spoke to David through Nathan. Read 2 Samuel 12:1-12. Who was the rich man in this parable? _____

David repented. Read 2 Samuel 12:13 and Psalm 51. You can see the consequences of his sin in 2 Samuel 12:14, 18a and Psalm 38. What were some of the consequences of David's sin? _____

_____

God forgave David and blessed him with another child–Solomon. Read 2 Samuel 12:24-25. Solomon was also known as Jedidiah which means *Beloved of the Lord*.

Take your piece of wood and hammer a few nails into it (far enough to make a hole, but able to be easily removed). If the wood represents your life, and the nails are sins you commit and allow to come into your life, then the holes are consequences of those sins. A sin is anything you do against God's law. When you repent, your sins are forgiven (1 John 1:9). They are thrown as far as the east is from the west (Psalm 103:12-13).

Remove the nails and lay them out of sight. Your wood is marred and scarred. even when God removes your sins, you must live with the scars and results. God applies His grace, and Jesus can give you victory even over all of the consequences (Romans 8:28).

David praised God (2 Samuel 22-23:7), and Solomon reigned after David's death and brought Israel to its Golden Age. In these verses, David claims God as whose rock, fortress, deliverer, God, refuge, shield, horn of salvation, stronghold, and savior? _____

Listen now to David's last words to Solomon. Read 1 Kings 2:2-4. If Solomon keeps God's laws, statutes, commandments, and testimonies, what will be Solomon's reward? _____
_____

What will be his sons' rewards? _____

More on King Solomon tomorrow.

You may not have committed adultery or murder, but it took all of Jesus' blood to forgive your pride, unbelief, faithlessness, and other *smaller* sins. With God, sin is missing the mark. Period. It doesn't matter if you missed His standard by an inch or a mile. We *all fall short* of God's holiness (Romans 3:23). If you were standing on a beach in Florida, and you wanted to jump to England, it wouldn't matter how far you could jump. Even the best long jumper in the world would still be hundreds of miles short of the English shore. This is how far we are from being able to reach God on our own.

God always welcomes a broken and contrite heart (Psalm 51). Repentance is the beginning of a long and successful relationship with your Creator and the Lover of Your Soul.

Questions to think about:

1. Jesus died for your sins. Does this include adultery and murder? Is He able to forgive all sins?

2. What was David's reaction to his sin? How do you react when you are confronted with your sin?

3. What consequences are you bearing because of sin?

4. Are you quick to repent when you have sinned?

5. Work on your memorized definition of wisdom.

    "Wisdom is the _____ to _____ correctly and use your _____ to avoid _____, solve _____, reach_____, and succeed _____ based upon _____."

6. Work on memorizing Proverbs 1:7.

    "The fear of the Lord is the _____ of _____; _____ despise _____ and _____."

Week 1 / Day 5

Solomon's Whole-Heartedness

The proverbs of Solomon the son of David, king of Israel ...
Behold I [God] have given you a wise and discerning heart,
so that there has been no one like you before you,
nor shall one like you arise after you.

Proverbs 1:1, 1 Kings 3:12

We are blessed with five sons. When God started throwing them at me two at a time, I quit! One of the twins got off of an airplane at age seven and declared he would grow up and be a pilot. I thought, "Yeah, sure. He will probably change his mind a hundred times before he is grown." I was wrong. This child never dreamed of anything else. He went through Civil Air Patrol as a teenager and experienced piloting and search and rescue. At age 17, he felt God was calling him to be a missionary. Having finished all of his flight classes, he is embarking on his last two years with the A&P (mechanical repair) classes and will graduate with a bachelor's degree in Missionary Aviation ready to fly for a missionary organization. He is single-minded and whole-hearted.

Solomon, the writer of Proverbs also did everything whole-heartedly. Read 1 Kings 2:12 and 4:20-28. You will find during Solomon's reign, Israel reached its height of power, land, riches, reputation, and peace. Find out why.

Read 1 Kings 3:1-15, 4:29-34. In 1 Kings 3:3 what was Solomon's motivation for obeying God?

_____

_____

In 1 Kings 3:9, what did Solomon ask of God? _____

_____

In verses 10-14, what was God's response? _____

_____

What was the condition God put upon His promise? _____
_____

Solomon's greatest earthly accomplishment was the building of a temple for God in Israel. Up to this time, God had dwelt in the midst of His people in a tent, a tabernacle. The presence of God rested upon the Ark of the Covenant kept within an inner room of the tabernacle called the Holy of Holies. Only the high priest was allowed in the presence of the ark, and then only once a year after many sacrifices. He would make a yearly sacrifice on the ark to God for the atonement of Israel's sins. Atonement is a covering up—the sacrifices covered up their sins. In 1 Kings 8:10-11, you will see God enters Solomon's temple to dwell or *tabernacle* there. At the dedication of this magnificent new temple, you will find Solomon's heart as he prays to God. Read 1 Kings 8:22-53.

In 1 Kings 8:22-24, Solomon first offers _____(vs. 23) to God. Then he asks God to keep His_____ (vs.25) and to have _____ (vs.28, 30, 32) upon the people and to _____(vs. 36) their sins.

In 1 Kings 8:40, how were the people to respond to God's just judgments and forgiveness? _____
_____

Solomon then blessed the people. Read 1 Kings 8:55-61. In 1 Kings 8:60, why was it so important the people walk in God's ways? _____
_____

According to verse 61, how much of your heart does God want? _____

God responds to Solomon with a promise and a warning (1 Kings 9:1-9).
In 1 Kings 9:4-5, what are the conditions of God's promise? _____
_____
_____

In 1 Kings 9:6-7, what would lead God to cut Israel off from the land and to destroy the nation?
_____
_____
_____

You will find even Solomon, with God's wisdom, falters and falls. Read 1 Kings 11:1-6.
What was Solomon's sin? _____
_____

He repents, but not before he, too, is told the consequences of his sins. Read 1 Kings 11:9-13. What are the consequences of his sin? _____
_____

Rehoboam was Solomon's son who became the next king of Israel. It was he the book of Proverbs refers to as *my son*. And yet with all that wisdom at his fingertips, he chose foolishness.

Read 1 Kings 12:1-16. This is where the kingdom of Israel was split into two kingdoms—the Northern Kingdom or Israel and the Southern kingdom or Judah. Wisdom is a choice!

An autobiography of Solomon's life, the book of Ecclesiastes, ends with great words of wisdom. In Ecclesiastes 12:9-14, what did Solomon conclude at the end of his life? _____

_____

Questions to think about:

1. Why do you obey God?

2. When you sin do you quickly ask God to forgive you?

3. Is there any sin too big for God to forgive?

4. Are you holding on to any areas of your heart (unforgiveness, bitterness, fear, control)?

5. In what areas of life are you living in your own power?

6. In what areas of life are you living in God's power?

7. Know your definition of wisdom.

   "Wisdom is the _____ to _____ correctly and use your _____ to _____ _____, _____ , _____ , and succeed _____ _____ based upon _____ ."

8. Keep working on memorizing Proverbs 1:7.

   The fear of the _____ is the _____ of _____ ; _____ despise _____ and _____ .

Week 1 Group Discussion

S ee the leader's guide at the back of this book for fill in the blank answers to the lessons and for a more thorough discussion of the questions below.

1. What is the difference between wisdom and knowledge? (Wisdom: Matt. 13:54, Luke 21:15, 1 Cor. 1:30, 1 Cor. 12:8. Knowledge: Phil. 1:9, Col. 2:3, James 1:5, Peter 1:2-3, 5-8, 3:18).

2. How does discernment relate to wisdom? (Phil. 1:9-11, Heb. 5:14).

3. How is your working definition of wisdom different than the world's view of wisdom? (1 Cor. 1:18-31, 2:6-10, 1 John 2:16-17).

4. What knowledge is biblical wisdom based on? (1 Cor. 1:18-31, 2:6-10).

5. Explain how the fear of the Lord is the beginning of wisdom. Relate this verse to your own life. (Fear: reverence, awe, giving God His proper place as Creator, King, Lord, Master: Ps. 111:10, Eccl. 5:6-7, James 3:7-8).

6. Why do you obey God? (John 14:15, John 15:10, Rev. 14:12).

7. Is there any sin too big for God to forgive? (David committed murder and adultery, the thief on the cross, Rom. 10:9-11, 1 John 1:9).

8. What should your reaction to sin be? (Ps. 51, 1 John 1:9, 2 Cor. 7:9-11).

9. How do you let God lead you rather than living in your own power? (Surrender, yield, Lordship, Prov. 3:5-6, Rom. 12:2, Eph. 4;1, 5:1, 4:14-15, 22-24).

10. Give examples from your life of using wisdom according to the definition. Recite together the working definition of wisdom and Proverbs 1:7.

The Beginning of Wisdom

The fear of the Lord is the beginning of knowledge;
Fools despise wisdom and instruction.

PROVERBS 1:7

The fear of the Lord is the beginning of wisdom;
A good understanding have all those who do His commandments;
His praise endures forever.

PSALMS 111:10

The fear of the Lord is the beginning of knowledge and wisdom. Proverbs was written from a father to his son to instill wisdom in his son's heart because Solomon, the father, wanted his son to make good and right decisions for his own life and for the nation of Israel. Good decisions based upon God's wisdom bring the fruit of righteousness and joy and peace. Solomon knew that these good decisions only come from a right relationship with God. In today's world of the New Testament (new covenant) through the blood of Jesus Christ, the only way that we can have a right relationship with God is through salvation based upon faith in Jesus.

David and Solomon were unable to walk perfectly before God, keeping His commandments, statutes, and testimonies and neither are we. Yet, without a wholehearted devotion to God, we are promised His curses, not His blessings of abundance. Here is where the marvelous, glorious, wonderful provision of God through Jesus comes in.

The beginning of knowledge and wisdom starts when God draws a human heart to Himself. After attaining some knowledge, that person reaches out to God and asks God for forgiveness and for God to be the controller of his life—will, mind, emotions, body, and spirit. When this happens this person is "born again" (John 3:7). Then and only then can a person establish a relationship with God and be allowed to come before the throne of grace. This is when the believer can begin to discern and apply God's wisdom found in His word.

Romans 3:10 claims, "There is none righteous, no not _____."

Romans 3:23 continues "_____ have sinned and fall short of the glory of God." Your God is holy (set apart and perfect). You cannot stand in His presence and have sin in your life.

Therefore, from the beginning of time, a blood sacrifice was required for the *covering up* of sins.
Romans 6:23 states, "The wages of sin is _____." We have all sinned, (literally meaning we have "missed the mark") and therefore, we all deserve death (eternal separation from God). The rest of that verse, however, brings hope and joy.

The second part of Romans 6:23 says, "But the _____ of God is eternal life in Christ Jesus our Lord."

Born of woman but not of man, Jesus did not inherit man's sinful nature or tendency passed down to all mankind through Adam. Jesus lived a perfect life, walking on this earth for approximately 32 years without sinning even once. He never sinned and therefore, He didn't deserve death. He, however, allowed Himself to be crucified so His blood would cover each of your sins. He was our substitute. He rose again on the third day and later ascended into heaven to sit at God's right hand. Now, when God sees me, He doesn't see my sin—it is covered up by Christ's blood.

What must I do to be saved? Romans 10:9-10 says, "If you confess with your mouth Jesus as Lord and believe in your heart that God raised Him from the dead, you _____." More than an insurance policy to keep you from hell and get into heaven, salvation gives you an avenue to have a relationship with God and is as significant as a new birth.

I became a Christian at the age of 13. My home life was chaotic and my siblings and I all reacted very differently. One day after a harsh revelation and concern for another family member, I made my way to the church I had been walking to and asked the Pastor for help. He said I would need to help myself before I could help anyone else. He asked me if I knew Jesus. I replied that I loved Him and read my Bible. That was all I knew to do. The pastor kindly led me to understanding my need to not only know about Jesus, but to know Him personally by confessing my sins and putting my life into God's hands going forth. I walked away that day with joy and hope and peace. I was a new creature, reborn, saved, and justified. (Justified—declared legally not guilty by the authority of God.)

Peter says in 1 Peter 1:3, "Blessed be the God and Father of our Lord Jesus Christ, who according to His great mercy has caused us to be _____ to a living hope through the resurrection of Jesus Christ from the dead, to obtain an inheritance which is imperishable and undefiled and will not fade away, reserved in heaven for you, who are protected by the power of God through faith for a salvation ready to be revealed in the last time."

To be *born again* denotes a change in your innate nature. You no longer are under the curse of a sin nature. You are now a child of the King of Kings with an eternal nature that is able to choose not to sin.

Read Romans 6:1-18. Salvation is a new birth, but in Romans 6:1 salvation is also a death. What are you to die to? _____

Baptism is a symbol of that death and new birth. According to Romans 6:4 what is the result of this death and birth? "So we too might walk in _____." Verse 7 is key. "For he who has died is _____ _____."

Verses 11-18 says you can be free from sin. Sin now longer has to be master over you. This comes from salvations first, then knowledge of God's word, prayer, and practice. You will make mistakes, but God is a good Father. He will set you back on your feet and let you try again (Psalm 37:23-24).

You were not saved and then left to your own devices. As a newborn baby needs nurturing, so does a new Christian. That nurture comes from God's word, prayer, and fellowship with other Christians. Not just a religion, Christianity is a relationship with a loving, heavenly Father and His family here on earth. Your eternity in heaven starts at the moment of salvation, not when you die. And an abundant life awaits those who are in Christ (John 10:10).

Questions to think about:

1. Put these verses in order as you would tell someone how to get to God.
    Romans 6:23b
    Romans 10:9-10
    Romans 3:23
    Romans 6:23a
    Romans 3:10

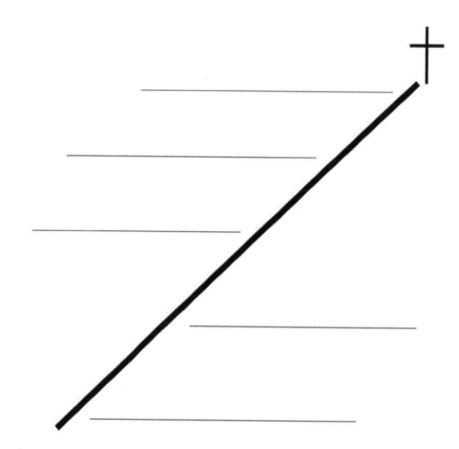

2. Have you accepted Jesus Christ as your Lord and Savior? Tell about that experience.

3. How has knowing Jesus changed your heart?

4. Who can you pray for and share the gospel of Jesus with using the Roman Road?

5. Keep memorizing Proverbs 1:7.

    "The _____ of the _____ is the _____ of _____; _____ despise
    _____ and _____."

God's Rules

Hear, my son, your father's instruction
And do not forsake your mother's teaching;
Indeed, they are a graceful wreath to your head
And ornaments about your neck.

PROVERBS 1:8

N oah Webster and George Washington both wrote notebooks full of rules to live by. These great men understood the necessity of giving themselves some boundaries for their behavior that would provide their lives with stability and allow them to reach their goals.

Some of George Washington's self-enforced rules are found in a small book called *Rules of Civility and Decent Behavior in Company and Conversation*.[3] His first recorded rule is, "Every action done in company ought to be some sign of respect to those that are present."

Some of his rules are common sense and others not so obvious. I especially like #9: "Spit not in the fire, not stoop low before it. Neither put your hands into the flames to warm them, nor set your feet upon the fire, especially if there be meat before it!

A very useful rule for those families with more than one child is #70: "Reprehend not the imperfections of others, for that belongs to parents, masters, and superiors."

And, lastly, #110, "Labour to keep alive in your breast that little celestial fire called conscience."

Many people think of the Bible as a rulebook with a list of *don'ts*. What they don't understand is these *don'ts* provide a hedge of protection. Just as a child is told, "Don't play in the street", and a teenager, "Don't smoke", the biblical *don'ts* keep us from harmful attitudes and actions that could scar us, maim us, or even kill us. God is not a holy killjoy. Just the opposite is true. He wants to bless us abundantly. He has preserved good things for His children. If we choose to live within His boundaries, He promises us peace, abundant life, and eternal life. He warns us, however, of the consequences of a life lived outside of His commands.

In order to keep in balance God's laws and judgments and God's love, grace, mercy, and provision, we must understand the difference between the Old and New Testaments (covenants). Proverbs was written before Christ. The Jews were under the laws of the Old Testament at this time. Therefore, Proverbs leans heavily towards God's laws. In the Old Testament (old covenant), God's promises and provisions for the nation of Israel were to be fulfilled here on earth with an earthly kingdom. The relationship with God was maintained through continual sacrifices of animal blood.

We have a better covenant through the blood of Jesus Christ. It is an eternal covenant. God's promises and provisions for us are for eternity which includes the life of the believer on earth and forever in heaven.

Proverbs was written for Israel under the old covenant of law, therefore the words set forth in Proverbs are principles not promises. These principles of wisdom have both earthly and eternal applications for the New Testament believer.

An example of eternal consequences is when we see evil people getting away with their evil deeds and living a life of luxury without seeming to pay for their actions. God says that He will judge all actions. Deuteronomy 32:35 says, "Vengeance is Mine, and retribution, in due time their foot will slip; for the day of their calamity is near, and the impending things are hastening upon them." Romans 12:19 reiterates this, "Never take your own revenge, beloved, but leave room for the wrath of God, for it is written, 'Vengeance is Mine, I will repay,' says the Lord." They may not get their dues here on earth, but there is a great judgment coming.

Read Romans 7:14-8:17.

Can you or any man keep all of the rules of the Old Testament or even just the 10 commandments? Yes or No? _____

Is trying your best and keeping most of the rules good enough to earn your way to heaven and give you a clear conscience? Yes or No? _____

Romans 8:1 is a key verse. "Therefore there is now no _____ for those who are in Christ Jesus."

We are to walk according to the Word of God, keeping the commandments and seeking to love God with all our hearts, mind, and soul. But we will make mistakes and sin.

1 John 1:9 says, "If we _____, He is faithful and just to forgive us of our sins and cleanse us from all unrighteousness."

Rules and principles are a blessing. They help us to know what is right and pleasing to our Lord and Savior. They keep us from having to suffer the consequences of ungodly and unwise actions.

List the top five rules you live by:

1.
2.
3.
4.
5.

Look up and define these words:

COMMANDMENTS:
LAWS:
STATUTES:
TESTIMONIES:

Read Psalm 19:7-14 and fill in the following chart.

God's Word	**Is what?**	**Accomplishing what?**
1. The law of the Lord	Perfect	Restoring the soul
2.		
3.		
4.		
5.		
6.		

Verse 10 continues to give worth to the Word of God. Scripture is more desirable than gold and sweeter than honey. It accomplishes two things: it warns God's servant and it brings great reward.

We can trust in God's Word, knowing it will produce in us all that is its essence—perfection, sureness, righteousness, purity, cleanness, and truth!

Questions to think about:

1. What rules did your parents give you as a child you did not understand at the time but later came to see as protection or provision.

2. God gave the rules in the Old Testament for five reasons. Read each of these reasons below and give an example of an OT rule that fits the first three.

   a. God's provision

   b. God's protection

   c. That we might know God's character.

   d. That we would realize that we could not keep the laws

   e. That we would realize that we needed a Savior

3. Look at the list of what God's Word accomplishes, and explain how one of these is being accomplished in your life.

4. Keep memorizing Proverbs 1:7. "The _____ of the _____ is the _____ of _____; _____ and _____."

Written to a Son

*My son, do not forget my teaching,
But let your heart keep my commandments.*

Proverbs 3:1

$\mathcal{N}$ow that you know who wrote the book of Proverbs, figure out to whom he wrote it. Who was Solomon's audience? Why did he take such pains to write his thoughts down?

Look first at Proverbs 1:8-10. To whom was Solomon writing? _____

Jot your answers down next to each verse. As you journey through Proverbs, be reminded again and again to whom the book was written.

Proverbs:

1:8	6:3
1:10	6:20
1:15	7:1
2:1	7:24
3:1	8:32
4:1	23:15
4:10	23:19
4:20	23:26
5:1	24:13
5:20	24:21
6:1	27:11

Now that you know to whom the book was written, dig deeper and discover why. Start by reviewing Proverbs 1:2-7. It seems important to this writer dad that his audience (his son) learn wisdom, instruction, discernment, and knowledge and be able to share it with others. The love of a father was the main motivator here. Solomon wanted to make sure his son was equipped to handle all that life might throw at him, because he loved his son. I truly believe God included this love letter in His Book to you for exactly the same reason—He loves you and wants you to experience the best of life. God is a Father writing to His children.

I am a mom. I would do anything including giving my own life that my children (and daughters-in-law and grand-children) would be saved and walk in trust and purity. If one of them had cancer and I had the cure, I would be proactive in making sure they understood and received that cure. I know the answer to sin and pride and depression and low self-esteem. The cure for these diseases is knowing Christ through salvation and then finding out more about Him through the word of God so they can be transformed and live lives of victory. I am proactive in reminding my children whom to turn to when they need answers, in giving them biblical advice and in urging them to seek God on their knees and to make time for Him. This is wisdom, and I want those I love to know wisdom through Jesus.

Look at Proverbs 2:1-5. The ultimate end of a man's search is to discern the fear of the Lord and to discover the knowledge of God. Continuing on in verses 2:6-22, Solomon reveals why this is so important. God will be a _____(vs.7) to those who walk with integrity, He will _____(vs. 8) the ways of His godly ones, He will _____(vs.12) you from the way of evil, and then you will live in the land and remain in it—heaven forever.

The following verses tell you some of the other reasons the author wrote these words for his son. Read each verse and write why Solomon wrote it to his son.

1:8-9 - _____

3:1-2 - _____

3:4 - _____

3:6 - _____

3:8 - _____

3:21 - _____

3:23 - _____

3:24 - _____

4:6 - _____

4:8 - _____

4:10 - _____

4:20 - _____

6:22 - _____

6:24 - _____

7:5 - _____

8:32 - _____

22:18 - _____

22:21 - _____

23:15 - _____

23:24-25 - _____

24:14 - _____

What promises! Based upon a father's love, a father's desire to see his son lead a long, successful, and satisfied life, these promises give hope. Just as this earthly father desired these joys for his son, how much more your heavenly Father wants you to be blessed with His abundance.

Questions to think about:

1. If you were a father or mother writing to your son or daughter, what advice would you give him/her?

2. What good advice did you receive from your parents? Be specific.

3. Keep memorizing Proverbs 1:5. "The _____ of the _____ is the _____ of _____; _____ despise _____ and _____."

4. You should have Proverbs 1:7 pretty much memorized by now. You are going to start on a longer portion of Scripture Proverbs 3:1-12. Don't worry. You will have until the end of this study to finish it, and you will be receiving help along the way. You will find these verses in Appendix C. For today, just read through these verses.

Definition of a Biblical Fool

Because they hated knowledge
And did not choose the fear of the Lord.
They would not accept my counsel,
They spurned all my reproof.

PROVERBS 1:29-30

In the next several lessons, you will be looking at a biblical fool and foolishness and a biblical wise man and wisdom. These are the foundations of the book of Proverbs.

First, you must understand the heart of a biblical fool. Draw your knowledge first from Psalm 14:1-3. It is interesting to note these verses are repeated by Paul in Romans 3:10-12 to describe the state of man *under sin* before being reconciled unto Christ. According to these verses what does a fool say in his heart? _____

_____

A biblical fool does not accept the authority of God. After he has made this declaration, he then acts corruptly. Sins committed does not make you a sinner, but rather your sin nature makes you sin for Jesus said in Matthew 15:18, "But the things that proceed out of the mouth comes from the _____ and those defile the man."

The person in my life who I would classify as a biblical fool does not know Jesus as his Savior. He is very angry, prideful, unforgiving, and has a very low self-esteem. He masks his insecurity with bravado and control. Do you know a biblical fool? _____ Are you one? _____

Keep in mind that only Christ was perfect. We all have areas in our lives where we still act foolishly. The good news is as you are made right in Jesus Christ, He convicts you of your foolish ways and helps you to overcome habits, ideas, and ways bound up in your old nature. If you notice a foolish action in Proverbs you still need help with, put a star beside the verse and begin praying that God will help you be an overcomer.

Turn to Appendix A and you will find a chart entitled *Foolishness: Characteristics and Results.* As you add to this chart over the following weeks, you will get a very good picture of a fool and the consequences of his foolishness.

Read the following verses and decide if the information contained in them is a characteristic of a fool or a result of his foolishness. List them under the correct heading. They do not have to be across from each other according to the verses. Just start at the top and make a list, jotting down key words or phrases. The first one has been done for you.

Proverbs:

1:7	1:16	1:29
1:11	1:18	1:30
1:12	1:19	1:32
1:13	1:22	

Questions to think about:

1. Explain this comment: Sins committed do not make you a sinner, but rather your sin nature makes you sin?

2. If that statement is true, then why must you be born again and not just forgiven?

3. Think of someone you know or someone famous who has the characteristics of a fool.

4. Begin memorizing Proverbs 3:1. If you learn with pictures, turn to Appendix C and draw pictures for *teaching* and *commandments*. (I drew a book and a set of stone commandments.) If colors help you more, you can highlight the words *teaching* and *commandments*. I also learn by doing, so making up some motions to go with the words can help as well.

Characteristics of a Fool

From the man who speaks perverse things;
From those who leave the path of righteousness
To walk in the ways of darkness;
Who delight in doing evil
And rejoice in the perversity of evil;
Whose paths are crooked,
And who are devious in their own ways.

PROVERBS *2:12-15*

Do you enjoy being around angry people who cause dissension and fear? According to Jan Silvious in her book, *Foolproofing your* Life[4], characteristics of a fool include the belief that he/she is always right, the use of anger to control, and trusting in his/her own heart. Throughout the book of Proverbs, you will see a fool is easily taken in by sin and refuses to put it aside thus becoming a stumbling block for others.

In Proverbs 1:10-19, you see that sin entices; it's fun for the moment. I love the verse in Hebrews describing Moses' choices: Hebrews 11:25 says, "Choosing rather to endure ill-treatment with the people of God than to enjoy the _____ of sin."

His motive was pure as seen in verse 26: "Considering the reproach of Christ _____ riches than the treasures of Egypt; for he was looking to the reward."

And that's really what Proverbs (and life) is about. It's about choices and taking responsibility for your own choices. Sin, for the moment, can be pleasurable and fun. I won't deny that. The third or fourth piece of fudge is good until I get a stomachache and add another pound!

But don't forget sin leads to _____ (Rom. 6:23 and James 1:14-15).

The break in relationship between you and God and the consequences you will experience in other relationships is not worth the short term excitement.

Using the metaphor of an adulteress to personify sin, sinfulness, Satan's deceptions, and the results thereof, Proverbs portrays God's jealousy of His relationship to His bride, the Church.

Read Proverbs 2:16-19, 5:3-6, 6:26-35, and 7:6-27 and fill in the blanks.

"For her house sinks down to _____
And her tracks lead to the _____."

"Her feet go down to _____,
Her steps take hold of _____[the grave]."

"The one who commits adultery with a woman is lacking sense;
He who would _____himself does it."

"So he does not know that it will cost him his _____."

These verses all state that adultery (friendship with the world) will lead to _____.

This metaphor of adultery was also used continuously by God to describe the nation of Israel as her heart turned from Him to the gods and idols of other cultures. Jeremiah 3:1-3 is one of a myriad of references where God compares His beloved children to harlots and adulteresses. This comparison is not limited to sexual relationships only (although this is certainly involved in Israel's unfaithfulness). Adultery applies to a heart condition of rebellion and self-gratification. An adulterer is one who makes a commitment to God and then chases after the things of this world.

Moses teaches the Israelites in Deuteronomy 6:5 to, "Love the Lord your God with _____ your heart and with _____ your soul and with _____ your might."

The pleasures of sin were enticing and their hearts were drawn away by the allure of riches, lands, freedom from rules, and all other forms of easy living. As you saw with Solomon, this did not (and does not) satisfy.

The fool in Proverbs, likewise, is drawn to the adulteresses' home and allured into sensual pleasures, thus forfeiting all the blessings of God and biblical living. You can't have it both ways. You must choose.

Add to your chart (Appendix A) the characteristics of foolishness and its results found in Proverbs:

2:16-19
5:3-6
6:26-35
7:6-27

Questions to think about:

1. Using Jan Silvious' definition of a fool, write about a time you acted the part of a fool. How could following Deuteronomy 6:5 have prevented those foolish notions?

2. The Bible states that God is a jealous God. How does this relate to the nation of Israel being an adulteress? How should this impact your life?

3. Praise God in prayer that even though you sometimes act the fool, you are forgiven.

4. Work on memorizing Proverbs 3:1-2. Highlight key words or add pictures for "length" (a ruler), "day" (a sun), "years" (a calendar), and "peace" (a peace sign).

My son, do not forget my _____,
But let your heart keep my _____;
For length of _____ and _____of life
And _____they will add to you.

Week 2 Group Discussion

1. Have you accepted Jesus Christ as your Lord and Savior? Tell about that experience. (John 3:15-17, Rom. 3:22-24, 6:23, 10:9-10).

2. How has knowing Jesus changed your heart? (Rom. 12:2, 2 Cor. 3:18, Eph. 4:14-15, Col. 3:15).

3. This is your test on the definition of wisdom. Recite it out loud: "Wisdom is …"

4. Discuss any rules your parents gave you that you did not understand at the time. (Deut. 8:5-6, Gal. 3:21-26, 4:1-2, Heb. 12:5-11).

5. Is there a rule in the Old Testament about which you have wondered why God gave it? (Deut.5:29, 8:6-7, Matt. 5:17-18, Rom. 7:12).

   In Numbers 19:2-9, I wondered why God told the Israelites to kill a heifer and burn it and place it outside the camp. Whenever someone touched something unclean, they were to go and wash their hands in this cow's burned ashes. Then I read *Little House on the Prairie5* Antibacterial soap is make from lard (animal fat) and ashes. The Israelites did not know about germs, but God did! What seemed unreasonable was really God's protection.

6. Look at the list of what God's Word accomplishes and explain how one of these is being accomplished in your life. Ps. 19:7-11, 119:11, Rom. 12:2, Col. 3:16, James 1:21).

7. Why is it important to know Proverbs is a letter from a father's heart to his son?

8. What good advice did you receive from your parents? Be specific.
   a. Explain this comment: sins committed do not make you a sinner, but rather your sin nature makes you sin. (Rom. 6:7, 6:11-14, 7:4-6, 7:1 - 8:1-8, Eph. 2:1-10, 2:5).

9. If that statement is true, then why must you be born again and not just forgiven? (John 3:7, Rom. 3:20-28, 4:5, 6:20-22, 2 Cor. 5:17, Gal. 6:15, 1 John 1:9).

10. Recite Proverbs 3:1-2.

Acquiring Wisdom

The beginning of wisdom is: Acquire wisdom;
And with all your acquiring, get understanding.
Prize her [Wisdom], and she will exalt you;
She will honor you if you embrace her."

PROVERBS 4:7-8

Turning to the uplifting, positive side of Proverbs, we will discuss wisdom. You are first introduced to wisdom in Proverbs 1:20-33. Read these verses.

In verses 20-23, is wisdom hiding and hard to find? _____

In verses 24-29, is wisdom hard to find? _____

Your reaction to wisdom makes the difference. This reminds me of a verse, Matthew 7:7.
What does this verse say you need to do to find Jesus, the All Wise One? _____
_____

James 1:5 also says to ask for wisdom and it will be given to you. According to this verse to what extent will God give you wisdom? _____

That's right, He will give wisdom generously.

Proverbs 1:33 is a key to finding happiness in this life. Sometimes life seems overwhelming because of the evil in the world around you. Just read the front page of the newspaper or watch the evening news and you will find evil in all its forms. But you can rest in the fact that if you seek wisdom, then you, "Shall live _____
_____ and will be at ease from the dread of evil" (Proverbs 1:33).

Here in Proverbs 1, you will find wisdom personified. You should not be surprised that she is actively seeking out those whose hearts will turn to her. A key to understanding wisdom is found in Proverbs 8:22-31. These verses describe Wisdom as one who was with God before the beginning of time, who was a master craftsman even as God formed our world. Before there were depths, this wisdom was brought or born forth (vs. 24). This wisdom was manifested in the flesh as Jesus Christ. John 1:1-5 says that He was with God from the beginning and all things came into being through Him. He is the only begotten of the Father (John 1:14). "Jesus came to seek and to save that which was lost" (Luke 19:10). It is inherent of God to want to call His children back to Himself and His life-giving laws. Wisdom (Jesus) seeks out those who will allow themselves to be drawn to her, those who will choose her paths. Your response to wisdom (Jesus) is the dividing line between foolishness and wisdom.

According to Proverbs 2:6 where does wisdom come from? _____

Look again at Proverbs 1:20-33. Wisdom promises you that if you but turn to her (Jesus), the Holy Spirit will be poured out upon you, and He will make His words known to you. According to verse 33, you will live securely and be at ease from the dread of evil. However, verse 24-32 tells you what happens to those who refuse her generous and free offer.

What are the consequences of not looking for wisdom? _____
_____

Proverbs 2:1-5 again reminds you that you must look for wisdom. In verse 2 you must, "Make your ear _____" and "Incline your _____." Verse 3 says you must, "Cry for _____ _____,_____ your voice for understanding." Verse 4 continues, "If you _____ her." Then in verse 5, "You will discern the fear of the Lord and _____ the knowledge of God."

Once again you see wisdom is not hidden if you seek her. God is not trying to make this difficult; He just requires you to be sincere and to look to Him for wisdom. Is God's wisdom different than that of man? Find the answer in 1 Corinthians 1:18-31.
Write verse 25 here: _____
_____

Proverbs 2:6-12, 20-21 gives you a brief glance at what can be yours if you but "Love the Lord your God with all your heart and with all your soul and with all your might" (Deut. 6:5).

List 12 things from these verses that are yours if you seek wisdom.

1.   7.
2.   8.
3.   9.
4.   10.
5.   11.
6.   12.

Wisdom bring the seven "P's".

God's...

        Presence

        Peace

        Power

        Provision

        Protection

        Purpose

        Patience

Turn to Appendix B entitled *Wisdom: Characteristics and Results*. Begin filling in your chart with these verses: Proverbs:

1:23	2:8	2:11	2:21
1:33	2:9	2:12	
2:7	2:10	2:20	

Questions to think about:

1. How does one seek wisdom?

2. Do you desire the results of wisdom you learned about today?

3. If your answer was "Yes", what step can you take today towards that end?

4. What blessings have you experienced because of your relationship with God?

5. Work on your memorization of Proverbs 3:1-3. (Add appropriate pictures or highlights.)

        My son, do not forget my _____,

        But let your heart keep my _____

        For length of _____and _____of life

        And _____they will add to you.

        Do not let _____and _____leave you;

        Bind them around your _____,

        Write them on the tablet of your _____.

Trusting God

Trust in the Lord with all your heart
And do not lean on your own understanding.
In all your ways acknowledge Him,
And He will make your paths straight.

PROVERBS 3:5-6

Today's and tomorrow's lessons will hone in on your memory verses: Proverbs 3:1-12. Proverbs 3 is a central passage to this incredible book. Containing the key to the mystery of how to live a biblical life, what the blessings of that life are, an understanding of God's correction, the priority of wisdom and God in your life, and even some practical advice. These verses are foundational to a trusting relationship with Christ.

Look first at this great mystery of how to live a biblical life. There are people all over our world today and in every generation past looking, searching, and seeking for the way to God. People are looking to put their trust in something. Every major religion—Hinduism, Islam, Confucianism, Buddhism, etc., as well as the major cults: Mormonism, Jehovah Witnesses, New Age, etc.—is looking for what men must do to be saved. In each of these religions, the answer is within man's power. If one prays hard enough, witnesses enough, does enough good works, meditates enough, or even gives up enough, then he/she will reach *god*. Islam promises heaven to those who die killing their enemies—Christians and Jews!

Christianity is the only religion stipulating that man's best is as filthy rags to God (Is. 64:6). Only in Christianity does one see, not man's work, but God's work as Jesus walked upon earth without sin and then died as a substitute for all of your sins. His last words? "It is finished!" You don't have to do anything else. Nothing more is required.

In Acts 16:30, some jailers asked Paul and Silas, "What must I do to be saved?" Their reply was, "_____ in the Lord Jesus, and you shall be saved."

That's it—no religious rituals or magic words! Ephesians 2:8 reiterates the work of salvation as a gift of God. "For by grace you have been saved through faith; and not of yourselves, it is a gift of God; not as a result of works, for no one should boast."

Jesus, Himself, says, "I am the Way, the Truth, and the life; _____ comes to the Father except through me" (John 14:6).

God the Father states many times in the Old Testament that He desires not your sacrifices, but rather your heart, broken and contrite before God (Ps. 51:16).

If you are believing in Jesus as Savior, but also as Lord, then you can trust in His promises, His provisions, His guidance, and direction and, in verses 11-12, His correction, reproof and discipline.
In Jeremiah 29:11, God proclaims His intentions. "'For I know the plans I have for you;' declares, the Lord, 'plans for _____ and not for calamity to give you a _____ and a _____.'"

I trust someone because their track record of keeping their word is good. God's track record is spotless. By reading stories in the Bible, of other Christians, and reflecting upon His faithfulness in your own life you will begin to see His pattern of trustworthiness. Can you think back to a time God was faithful in your life? It might have been before you even recognized Him or His Hand? _____

_____

Fear is the opposite of trust. To walk in trust requires you to face your fears and realize God is bigger than any situation or person that puts fear in your heart. Turn your circumstances over to God, trust Him to prove Himself faithful, and refuse to worry or fret (Ps. 37:1-2).

A few years ago, I was lying in bed in severe pain. I had already had four spinal surgeries and was headed to another one. I complained to God praying, "I can't do this anymore. I can't do this for another 20 years, another 10 years, another year, another month, another week, another day!" In that clear, small voice God responded, "I didn't ask you to. I ask you to endure right now and I am with you" (Prov. 27:1, Matt. 6:34). That was the day I gave my future over to God and He became the Lord of my future as well as my past and present. He didn't take away the pain. I now have had six spinal surgeries. But each day is glorious lived in His presence. I have learned to trust and appreciate all God has allowed me to do. I will be healed; it just might not happen until eternity!

Trusting in God is not a blind faith but rather faith in One who is able, who has the capacity to deliver, and who desires what is very best for you. You receive an understanding of God your Father from doing what Proverbs 3:1-4 commands—by knowing His Word, keeping His Word, memorizing His Word (binding it around your neck, writing them on the tablets of your heart). Then you open the channel of relationship and blessings between man and God. God desires not your works but your heart (Jer. 24:7, Deut. 4:29). And to top it off, this life of trust is spent with the blessings of Jesus.

See what blessings you can find in Proverbs 3:1-10. (I found 10.) What a good and mighty God we serve!

Isaiah 30:15 helps me to center on resting and trusting in God. It shows how God's wisdom is different than man's wisdom. "In _____ and _____ you will be saved, In _____ and _____ is your strength."

My first instinct when things are out of control or I'm overwhelmed is to get busy. Resting at such a time is counter-intuitive. I have been at a place several times in my life where I didn't have a choice. I was born with a form of spina bifida and have lived in chronic pain all of my life having undergone six major spinal surgeries as an adult. Each recovery has been one to two years in duration. Many have been the days when I couldn't get out of bed. The laundry still needed to be done, the meals fixed, the boys taught (we homeschooled), and the housework kept up. I could do nothing. I could worry and fret or I could trust God, rest in Him, and remain joyful and encouraging in the midst. I chose the latter, and we all made it through with little frustration. The boys learned household skills and their wives love me for it! They also learned compassion, servanthood, and patience.

Questions to think about:

1. Jesus' last words were, "It is finished." What things, other than Jesus' death and resurrection, are you trusting as part of your salvation?

2. Do you seek God's blessings or a trusting relationship with God?

3. In difficult times, which of the two choices in question two will see you through with your faith intact?

4. Have you been through a hard situation, prayed that God would change your circumstances, and found His answer to be no? Share that experience.

5. How was He still faithful in this?

6. Have you given your future to God?

7. Think about the verse Isaiah 30:15. This is actually a good definition of trust. Do you tend to rest and trust in a difficult situation or do you tend to worry and fret?

8. What does God say about worry? Look at Philippians 4: 6-7.

9. Is worry sin?

10. Work on memorizing Proverbs 3:1-8.

Blessings and Curses

My son, do not reject the discipline of the Lord
Or loathe His reproof,
For whom the Lord loves He reproves,
Even as a father corrects the son in whom he delights.

Proverbs 3:11-12

ontinuing on with the rich wisdom of Proverbs 3, begin by looking at verses 11-12. Read these verses. These are not easy verses, but, oh the blessing because even discipline is in God's character. Discipline definitely includes correction and punishment but also embraces the idea of loving guidance. Reproof is the reminder of the wrong and the way to correcting that wrong. Both can be gentle, or both may require punishment and/or a harsh attention-getting circumstance. It all depends upon how responsive your heart is to correction.

Take a minute and look at Deuteronomy. These passages are so foundational to understanding God's desire to bless, but also His right to discipline His people.
Read Deuteronomy 4:1-10.

In verses 1, 6, 10, Why did God give the Israelites statutes and judgments? _____
_____

Read 4:11-20. Verses 15 and 19 contain two warnings. What are they?

_____
_____

Read 4:21-28. Verse 24 describes God as a _____ God.

Jealousy is thought of as a bad trait. But in this situation jealousy is a wonderful characteristic of a holy God. God will not stand by and allow His followers to share their worship and devotion with false gods. He wants your whole heart, not just a little bit. The Christian Romans who so often sacrificed their lives during the time of the Caesars did so not because of their worship of Jesus, but because of their exclusive worship of Jesus. The Romans wouldn't have minded if they had set their God up on the mantle along with the Roman gods, or if they had bowed to Jesus along with bowing to Caesar. The early Christians, however, would bow and worship God and God alone, and so they were martyred.

Moses gives the Israelites a warning in verses 25-28. They will be guilty of what sin? _____

What will be their punishment? _____

Read Deuteronomy 4:29-39. What great promises! Verse 29 says you can find God!

What must you do to find God? _____

Verse 30 prophesies that the people will return to God and will _____ to His voice.

Verse 31 states that your God is a compassionate God. What will He remember? _____
_____

Verse 36 shows the compassion of God by reminding the Israelites of God's discipline. That discipline was to lead the Israelites to know the truth of verse 39. "The Lord, He is God in heaven above and on the earth below; _____ ."

Read Deuteronomy 4:40. What is the provision of verse 40? _____
_____

What condition must be met in order to gain these things? _____
_____

Now turn to chapter 6 of Deuteronomy. This chapter is titled in my Bible as *Obey God and Prosper*. Read this entire chapter, but focus on verses 4-7, 13, and 18. Verses 4-5 are part of the Jewish *Shema*. These are verses found in Deuteronomy and Numbers that are repeated several times a day by the Jewish leaders and faithful Jews as part of their liturgy.

Why do you think they chose these two verses as a part of such an important tradition?
_____
_____

What do these two verses mean to you?

_____

_____

_____

Verse 6 and 7 say how important these verses are to God. He wants them not just written down or read daily, but to be imprinted upon your heart—to be memorized, thought about, and acted upon. Then, they are to be taught to your children diligently. Not understanding this at the time, the Jewish nation religiously followed verses 8-9 and wore boxes (called phylacteries) on their foreheads with these verses tucked inside and set them into boxes by their doors and touched them when entering and exiting, but they didn't put them into the deep recesses of their hearts. It's kind of like a spelling assignment where you were asked to write each word 20 times. The teacher was not really interested in that sheet of paper which had the words on it; she was using the writing as a device to get the words into your brain. God was using the boxes as reminders of what needed to be put into their hearts.

Verse 13 further explains God's requirements. What three things were the Israelites to do?

_____

_____

If they upheld their end of the covenant, what did God promise (vs. 18)? _____

_____

Now turn over to chapter 11. This chapter further tells of the rewards of obedience. Notice God reminds the Israelites of His discipline in verse 2. Which of these verses remind you of the Shema? _____

_____

Just a few more passages to go. Turn to Chapter 28:15-68. Here you will find the consequences of disobedience.

List the curses that will come because of disobedience. (I found more than 30.)

And, lastly, look at Deuteronomy 30:1-3. What was the purpose of God's discipline? _____

_____

God still disciplines today. Discipline might come through illness, loss, broken relationship with Him, consequences of your actions, lack of direction, and many other disturbing things. But whatever the discipline, it is always from the hand of a loving and compassionate God who desires above all else that you might turn back to Him and love Him with all of your heart, soul, and might.

Through life's hard moments you will see God's grace (Deut. 30:1-3). Remember the rules God laid down for His people when at Mt. Sinai? You learned in this lesson that God's rules are a hedge about you to keep you from harm. But God gave you free will. If you choose to step outside of God's hedge of protection by doing something sinful, having an attitude of rebellion, or refusing to confess and repent, He will discipline you to bring you back into fellowship with Himself.

God, as your Father, delights in you says Proverbs 3 verse 12. Your response to God should be obedience, love, respect, and a desire to be with Him and to please Him. That's where wisdom comes in (again). Verses 13-20 should remind you of wisdom and her rewards. Finding how to please God and how to respond to God is all wrapped up in understanding who God is – His attributes, His character, His desires, and His heartbeat. You should seek for this wisdom (found within Scripture and through prayer) diligently.

It should be utmost in your mind. "For what will a man be profited, if he gains the whole world, and forfeits his soul" (Matt. 16:26)? Wisdom's gain is better than jewels, gold, or silver. She is life itself! Verses 19-20 should remind you again of the inability to separate Jesus and wisdom. Wisdom was the very power of creation, as Jesus formed the universe. That same wisdom will be your provision, protection, and even your confidence.

Sometimes when our circumstances look bleak, it seems as if we are under God's curses rather than His blessings. God does discipline and prune His children. God corrects us lovingly through His word. He does not use His word to beat us down, but rather to correct our errors in thinking so that we can realize His blessings. God disciplines us when we have an attitude or action that is not in line with God's holiness because it keeps us from fully fellowshipping with God.

Discipline is a response to our sin. God prunes us to purify our hearts that we might bear more fruit. Pruning includes cutting away anything that is superfluous or unnecessary in our lives that will keep us from bearing more fruit in our own lives and for the kingdom of God. Pruning can feel like discipline. Ask God to show you any sins. If you have confessed every sin and have a clear conscience before God, then you can assume that He is pruning you.

Questions to think about:

1. Remember a time you were punished and are now glad that you received that punishment. Refer to Romans 8:38.

2. Remember a time you were punished when you thought the punishment was unjustified or too harsh.

3. Did you change your heart or actions in either one of the instances of #1 or #2?

4. Sometimes God is not punishing you but rather pruning you through the tough circumstances of life. How is pruning different than punishment?

5. Work on memorizing Proverbs 3:1-3. Begin adding verse 4.

My _____, do not forget my _____,
But let your _____ keep my _____;
For _____ of _____ and _____ of life
And _____ they will add to you.
Do not let _____ and _____ leave you;
_____ them around your _____,
_____ them on the tablet of your _____.
So you will find favor and good repute
In the sight of God and man.

Choosing Wisdom

I have directed you in the way of wisdom,
I have led you in upright paths...
Take hold of instruction; do not let go.
Guard her, for she is your life.

PROVERBS 4:11, 13

Read Proverbs 3:13-26. According to verse 14, whose profit is better than silver and whose gain is better than fine gold? _____

Do you think the majority of people in today's world would agree with this statement? Why or why not?

_____

_____

Upon reading verse 15, you might disagree, thinking there are things in this world that you desire more than God's wisdom: popularity, friends, a spouse, children, appearance, to be smarter at your job or in school, an opportunity to attend college, different skills, etc.

What are your desires? _____

_____

Right now all those things seem most important, but the truth is when you gain God's wisdom it will include the right priority for all those things. God may choose to bless you with your desires, or He may not. But when you have stood before God in prayer and trusted Him and known the joy that comes from being in His presence, all these things will not seem so important. When you truly grasp the reality that you are a child of the King, an heir to heaven, and can sit upon His lap and talk to God, then you will have gained wisdom and all the treasures of earth will dim in comparison. God will then put His desires in your heart (Ps. 37:4).

The 7 byproducts of seeking God are listed in Proverbs 3:16-18. List them below:

1.
2.
3.
4.
5.
6.
7.

Verses 19 and 20 remind you why Christ is to be your unmovable foundation. He is timeless and eternal. His wisdom is from before time and will be after time. Upon God's wisdom alone can you stand no matter your culture, your nation, your era.

Where do you find this wisdom? God's Word, first of all. The Bible is inexhaustible, therefore this study, as well as any Bible study, is just a guide. God's depth cannot be reached, but it is okay to dive down deep again and again to gain more of his treasures. Don't read the Bible through and then stick this wisdom on the shelf as another book accomplished.

"God's Word is _____ and _____ and sharper than any two-edged sword" (Heb. 4:12). We need to read it, memorize it, think about, pray through it, and read it again.

Read 2 Timothy 3:16-17. What four actions is Scripture profitable for?

1.
2.
3.
4.

What is the reason given for these actions in vs. 17? _____
_____

Proverbs 3:24-26 gives you some benefits from choosing wisdom. Put them on your wisdom chart in Appendix B. (I found 10.)

Another source of God's wisdom is reading biographies of men and women of faith through the ages. As you see God interact and respond to their prayers and faithfulness, your own faith will soar. As you see men and women humble themselves and walk according to God's Word, you will see them triumph over great odds. They were not always the richest, the prettiest, the most popular, etc., but they were at peace, used by God, and looking forward to an eternity with God.

Missionary stories, stories of martyrs of the faith, and great leaders in ministry can round out your literary heritage. The following are among my favorite giants of the faith.

Joni Erickson-Tada is a woman who became a quadriplegic at age 17 and went on to start a ministry encouraging other disabled individuals and getting laws passed to enable them to function easier in society such as ramps and accessible restrooms. She is an amazing artist using her teeth to hold her pencil, a beautiful singer in spite of her lowered lung capacity, an author and a speaker.[6]

Corrie Ten Boom was a survivor of the Nazi concentration camps of WWII. She and her family were caught hiding Jewish refugees in their home. She was an inspirational speaker and author—a prayer warrior and a faithful follower of Christ in spite the deaths of many of her family members.[7]

Watchman Nee was a Chinese pastor who taught by asking questions and wrote many wonderful books. In 1922, he initiated church meetings in Fuzhou that may be considered the beginning of the local churches in China. My favorite book of his is *Sit, Walk, Stand* which walks the believer through the book of Ephesians.[8]

George Mueller was a Christian evangelist and the director of an orphanage in Bristol, England. He cared for 10,024 orphans during his lifetime and provided educational opportunities for the orphans He established 117 schools which offered Christian education to more than 120,000 children. He was a man of prayer who often relied upon the Lord for providing the next meal, the next building, and the next direction.[9]

Bruce Olsen was a young man who had a passion for missions. Having been turned down by several mission organizations, he boarded a plane to Venezuela and converted the Motilones, a violent stone-age tribe. Through physical perils, illness, betrayal, and lack of support, he lived among the Motilones and taught them about God.[10]

Brother Andrew was a Christian missionary famous for his exploits smuggling Bibles to communist countries in the height of the Cold War, a feat that has earned him the nickname "God's smuggler."[11]

Jim Elliot and Nate Saint were martyred by the Auca Indians of Ecuador as they tried to reach this cannibalistic tribe for Jesus.[12] Jim's wife, Elisabeth Elliot later returned to the tribe and many were brought to salvation through Christ.

These men and women chose the narrow gate of Matthew 7:13-14. "Enter by the narrow gate, for the gate is wide and the way is broad that leads to_____, and many are those who enter by it. For the gate is small and the way is narrow that leads to _____, and few are those who find it."

You enter in through the gate of wisdom and truth of the Scriptures. You can bet your life on them. I would emphasize here, again, salvation is not through works. When Jesus said, "It is finished," He, and He alone accomplished your salvation. However, salvation and love for your Savior will lead you to walk in a way that pleases God. God actually changes your heart and desires to make you want to live your life in a God-pleasing way (Ps. 37:4 and 2 Cor. 5:17). He transforms your purposes, goals, expectations, and your very essence when you renew your minds daily by abiding in Christ Jesus (Rom. 12:2). These verses in Proverbs then are a gift from God as they tell you how to live in order to please God. Your own heart gives testimony to these words as you study them, live them, and reap the benefits and blessings of your God. The way, however, is narrow. Many of these life principles are not popular in today's culture. To live them out may require you to buck society, to say no to pleasure, pride, luxuries, and friends. In the end, God promises you eternal life, and for now, peace, a relationship with God, and His guidance—a life and walk of faith. It's hard. It's lonely sometimes. But, it's worth it.

Turn to your Wisdom chart and put in verses 13-26.

Questions to think about:

1. In what ways have you decided to go God's direction rather than the world's?

2. How has God given you the strength to go against the flow?

3. Work on memorizing Proverbs 3:1-3.

My _____ , do not _____ my _____ ,
But let your _____ my _____ ;
For _____ of _____ and _____ of _____
And _____ they will _____ to you.
Do not let _____ and _____ you;
_____ them _____ your _____ ,
_____ them on the _____ of your _____ .
So you will find _____ and good _____
In sight of _____ and man.

Doing Good Deeds

Do not withhold good from those to whom it is due,
When it is in your power to do it.

Proverbs 3:27

℟ ead Proverbs 3:27-30.

Today you will begin with what I call the practical advice section of Proverbs. What a deep well of suggestions for putting your faith to work in your day to day life!

Start with verse 27. "Do not withhold good from those to whom it is due, when it is in _____ _____ to do it."

This flows from the love of Christ in you. If you are grounded in God's Word and abiding in Him moment by moment, the fruit of the Spirit (Gal. 5:22) will flow freely in your life. I have never seen a tree struggling and laboring to push fruit out of its limbs. Rather, a tree puts its roots deep into the ground and takes in water and nutrition and the fruit is a natural by-product. In the same way, you are to be rooted in the Word of God and drinking the Living Water and eating the Word daily. Naturally, from out of your being, will grow the fruits as evidence of your faith and trust. Begin looking for opportunities to bless others. A good deed done in secret without expecting any return blesses the recipient as well as the giver.

My husband managed an apartment complex while in college. We were not yet married, but I learned from him that he desired to replant a flowerbed at the apartments the next day. A girlfriend and I snuck up to the apartments at midnight and planted a garden for him. Imagine his surprise the next morning when he stepped outside ready for a couple of hours of work and was greeted with bright, colorful marigolds and cheerful daffodils!

Choose two people who you can do something special for just because it is in your power to do it.

Person 1:   Who?

             What?

Person 2:   Who?

             What?

Now look at verse 28. This verse follows in the vein of verse 27. A look at Deuteronomy 24:15 will help to clarify this verse. If someone is withholding what rightly belongs to another, he is harming the other and causing doubt and anxiety. This can become a source of power that people misuse. They feel that by having another's possessions, they can manipulate and rule to their advantage. This is not a God honoring attitude. If you finish each day's business with others by the end of each day, both parties are free to move on. And you are free to go before the Lord with a clear conscience and wait upon His bidding.

Now finish up with verses 29 and 30. Abiding by what you learned in verse 27, you naturally avoid devising harm or contending with a neighbor without cause.

1 Thessalonians 4:11 tells you to "Make it our ambition to lead a quiet life and attend to your _____ _____ and work with _____."

There is a right time to contend or confront another but not without cause. Proverbs 25:21-22 says, "If your enemy is hungry, _____ food to eat; and if he is thirsty, _____ _____ water to drink; For you will heap burning coals on his head, and the Lord will _____ _____you." God will reward your kindness. The heaping of coals on your enemy's head may lead him to seek forgiveness or restitution or at least make him be a bit nicer to you.

Add these verses to your wisdom chart (Proverbs 3:27-30).

Questions to think about:

1. Tell about a time when you blessed someone anonymously.

2. Tell how you felt when you did something for someone else anonymously.

3. Tell how you feel when someone goes out of their way to do something nice for you.

4. Be ready to recite Proverbs 1:1-4.

Week 3 Group Discussion

1. Think about the verse Isaiah 30:15. This is actually a good definition of trust. Do you tend to rest and trust in a difficult situation or do you tend to worry and fret? (Ps. 56:11, Matt.11:28-30).

2. Jesus' last words were, "It is finished." What things, other than Jesus' death and resurrection, do you try to make part of your salvation? (Phil. 3:7-11, Rom. 10:4, 11:6).

3. Do you seek God's blessings or a relationship with God? Why? (Rom. 8:15-16, Eph. 1:3-6).

4. What blessings have you experienced because of your relationship with God?

5. Sometimes God is not punishing you but rather pruning you through the tough circumstances of life. How is pruning different than punishment? (John 15:1-5, 2 Tim. 3:16-17).

6. In what ways have you decided to go God's direction rather than the world's? (Gal. 5:19-21, James 4:4, 1 John 2:15-16).

7. How has God given you the strength to go against the flow? (Ps. 28:7, Is. 30:15, 1 Cor. 10:14, 1 Peter 4:11).

8. Tell about a time when you blessed someone anonymously. (Luke 6:28, John 13:14-17, Romans 12:14).

9. Who did you surprise this week with a good deed? What did you do?

10. Recite Proverbs 3:1-4.

Choices and Consequences

> How blessed is the man who finds wisdom
> And the man who gains understanding.
> For her profit is better than the profit of silver
> And her gain better than fine gold.
> She is more precious than jewels
> And nothing you desire compares with her.
> Long life is in her right hand;
> In her left are riches and honor.
>
> PROVERBS 3:13-16

You will begin to notice that much of Proverbs is written in two line sayings. These sayings are called couplets. There are three basic types of couplets you will encounter throughout the book of Proverbs. The first kind is the most used—opposites. These couplets state a principle in the first line and give an opposite statement in the second, but the two lines never contradict each other. Some examples of this type of couplet are Proverbs 3:33-35. Verse 35 says, "The wise will inherit honor, but fools will display dishonor."

You will discern two different attitudes—wise and foolish and two different outcomes—honor and dishonor. This type of couplet always leaves the reader with a very clear cut choice. Do I want honor or dishonor? Then do I need to act wisely or foolishly? Look at verses 3:31-35. You'll learn about the other two types of couplets in later lessons.

Fill out the following chart:

	ATTITUDE	OUTCOME	ATTITUDE	OUTCOME
vs. 32	crooked man	abomination	upright	intimacy with God
vs. 33				
vs. 34				
vs. 35				

Add these verses to your foolish and wise charts (Appendixes A and B).

Look at Proverbs 3:31: "Do not envy a man of violence, and do not choose any of his ways."

At first glance you might say "Why would I envy a violent man in the first place?" Many envy the adventure, excitement and riches of such a lifestyle. Not all, but some men of violence seem to have it all—the house, the cars, the fame, the fun. It's the popular boys and girls who have all the friends and seem to break all the rules.

Read Psalm 10. This is a description of how you see reality, but remember God is bigger and sees the whole picture all the way to the end and His judgments will stand forever.
Now flip back a Psalm and look at Psalm 9:7-10. Will the riches of the wicked stand forever? No! What will stand forever? _____

In verse 8, the Word proclaims that God's judgment will be done in righteousness and with _____.
This means He will not play favorites. Each of us will be judged based upon whether we accepted Jesus Christ as our Savior.

Verse 10 is a promise you can stand on. Write this verse out below.

_____

_____

_____

Proverbs 3:32: For the _____ man is an abomination to the Lord; But He is intimate with the

_____.

In this verse you are introduced to the *crooked man*—the man whose ways are not right and straight forward before the Lord. This man is an affront, an abomination before the very God who created him. Abomination is a very strong word. It is not something that merely disgusts but something that utterly repulses. A crooked man utterly repulses God. The creature God made to love and draw to Himself has become an abomination to its very Creator. Many would say, "Oh, I'll get things right with God later." But later may never come, and that one would die utterly repulsive to God to be put away from Him for eternity. Even if such a one does turn to God later, it will be with many regrets. For even though God's mercy is greatest, man must live with the consequences of his actions. One of those consequences is often a hardened heart—a heart which would not hear God and obey.

But, the opposite is also true. God is intimate with the upright. As a believer you have access to the very throne of God (Heb. 4:16). He knows your heartbeat and you know the very mind of Christ (1 Cor. 2:16). He desires an intimate relationship with you. When you are walking uprightly as His child, you will desire intimacy with God. But how you can run and hide when you know you have sinned just as Adam did in Genesis 3:9-10. That intimate relationship can be restored once again by confession as read in I John 1:9. Write this verse out here:

_____

_____

Wow! To be intimately known by God! You can know you are moving toward God when your desire is not for God's benefits but, rather, for God Himself.

Do you desire God's blessing, protection, provision, mercy, and love, or do you desire Him?_____ When we desire God more than His blessings, we will receive His many blessings in abundance.

Pray a prayer of praise to God for He knows and loves you.

Proverbs 3:33 says, "The curse of the Lord is on the house of the _____, But He blesses the dwelling of the _____."

God is the same yesterday, today, and forever (Heb. 13:8). Although God, as revealed in the New Testament, is a God of love and mercy, He is still a God of justice as revealed in the Old Testament. Even in the Old Testament, God shows great mercy and faithfulness and has such a desire to bless His children. However, He is a holy God who cannot stand before sin. Therefore, God curses sin and the sinner, not out of perverse anger, but out of a heart of tough love. If it takes a curse to turn some towards God, then God will oblige. The curse is used as a hedge to give man direction and consequence. Studying Deuteronomy is very eye-opening to understanding God's heart within the scope of His curses and blessings.

Take a moment and glean over Deuteronomy chapters 6-8 and 28 and 29:15-20.

It is all summed up in Deuteronomy 29:15-20. God wants to bless. But since He gave you a free will to choose, He sets out for you the option of His curses (if you so choose) in order that you might turn back to Him.

This is an important principle to remember if you have children. They are wonderful, of course, but they will disobey. You can take their disobedience as a personal affront and get angry or you can set up a system of blessings and curses (disciplinary actions). The best way to discipline as a parent is to be like a police officer, emotionally detached, but meting out prearranged consequences. In our home we found the best incentives to be poker chips. Each child had his own color. We went out and bought a *store*—several desirable items of various cost and we put price tags on them to be redeemed by poker chips. One Mom I shared this with took her daughter clothes shopping and then came home, hung them all in a closet and tagged them. Her daughter then had to earn them back. We included getting to have a date with Mom or Dad, getting to have a friend over, as well as toys, roller blades, etc. It is a great way for the children to learn about immediate gratification or saving for the big prize.

Each child made a "token" bucket and we set the rules down in writing on a poster board pinned to the living room wall. Some of our rules included doing chores with a smile and good attitude, remembering our manners, or doing extra nice things for a sibling. All of these actions deserved tokens. On the other hand, tokens could be taken away for hitting, yelling, disrespect, etc. The key to the system is to be consistent and to have prearranged consequences. We wrote offenses and consequences on a poster board in the living room. If someone got in trouble I sent them to the poster to read their punishment. The child would be mad at the poster, not at me, and I didn't have to keep coming up with consequences. You can always add some as they crop up. The overriding rule should be, "If it didn't make your brother feel special, then it's wrong!"

Also notice in this verse, what is cursed or blessed—the house, the dwelling place. Your decisions, choices, and actions affect not only yourself, but all of those within your family. This is true of not only the husband and wife, but also the children. Each of us has an option of being a curse or a blessing; and it all depends on your choices to be wicked or upright before the Lord.

Read Proverbs 10:1. This is a great verse to memorize. Are you are blessing or a curse in your home or with your family? _____We all are both sometimes.

Write about a time when you were a blessing: _____
_____

Write about a time when you were a curse: _____
_____

You have the option, the choice is yours to make daily, hourly, minute by minute.

Questions to think about:

1. Which life is more real—this earthly one or your eternal one? Explain.

2. What riches should we seek?

3. How are God's curses used to bless?

4. In the Old Testament, was God angry and unforgiving or patient and faithful?

5. Work on memorizing Proverbs 1:1-6. Add pictures to verses 5-6 in appendix A

Grace/Mercy, Honor/Dishonor

Though He scoffs at the scoffers,
Yet He gives grace to the afflicted.

PROVERBS 3:34

A scoffer is equivalent to a proud man—one who thinks he knows everything and yet understands so little. Shaking his fist at God, the scoffer is the man who says, "I can live my own life; I don't need You!" He scoffs at God's wisdom to give good gifts and instead tries to horde up earth's treasures. He laughs at loving his enemies; rather, he seeks revenge. God will shake His head at such a one.

"Yet", the Word says, "God gives grace to the afflicted." What is grace? It is best described along with God's mercy. Mercy is not getting what you deserved (death, separation from God), whereas grace is getting what you don't deserve (God's love, intimacy, forgiveness). It often takes circumstances beyond your control, a disaster, a personal battle, a physical, emotional, relational breakdown before you stand before God and say, "I can't do life on my own, I need God." And God's grace is then poured down upon His child.

Paul, the great apostle of the New Testament cried out to God in his affliction three times (2 Cor. 12:7-10). God's response was not taking the affliction out of Paul's life, but rather, He replied, "My _____ is _____ for you." God wanted Paul to keep the affliction and lean on God rather than for God to heal him and for Paul to lean on himself. Yes, God can and does heal, but He is a sovereign God who knows what's best for each of us, and sometimes you need His grace more than you need to be delivered from your affliction.

Physical suffering is an affliction; others include difficult people in your life, changes, loss, and confusion about a situation. God's grace brings peace in the midst of the storm, the comfort of His presence, full knowledge of His forgiveness, and acts as a balm or salve to soothe the emotions of your afflictions.

God's grace brings peace in the midst of the storm, the comfort of His presence, full knowledge of His forgiveness, and acts as a balm or salve to soothe the emotions of your afflictions.

What do your afflictions bring: grace or prideful independence? _____

Try leaning on God and being bathed by His grace.

Proverbs 3:35:

> The wise will inherit honor,
> But fools display dishonor."

Honor: respect and distinction, great privilege, esteem; to be thought well of and to have a good reputation; to gain favor with God and man (Luke 2:52).

Wow! Sounds great! How do you get it? By being wise.

Write the definition of wisdom from lesson one. _____

_____

_____

Simply put: Live God's way and gain honor. Live your way and receive dishonor.

How do you know God's way? It's all written down for you in God's Instruction Book—the Bible. You are to "meditate on it day and night" (Ps. 1:2).

Are you having daily time reading God's Word? _____

My daily quiet time changed drastically one day when my oldest boys were two and three-years old. I often found myself impatient and yelling at these two precious treasures. Yelling was the example of my childhood home and had become an unwelcome habit in my own life. I posted verses all over our apartment about anger. I memorized them and prayed them out loud. I kept begging God to take away this anger. One day I heard that still small voice as I prayed. God said, "You are praying amiss. Don't pray I take the anger and yelling away from you, rather pray I fill you up with so much of Me there is no room for the anger." That was the day I quit having my quiet time and setting my Bible and my faith on the shelf for the rest of the day. That was the day I began practicing the presence of God throughout each day praising Him in song as I worked, speaking aloud to the boys of His magnificent creation as we walked or drove, and reading His word every chance I got.

You can know God's way through prayer and Bible study. You and your best friend enjoy spending time together learning about each other. You talk, and you listen. You learn God's way the same way. You talk to Him, and you listen.

Do you spend daily time in prayer speaking and listening? _____

A third way to know God's way is to read about good and bad examples from history. We've already talked about some of the good ones, but here are few rotten apples you can learn from as well: Hitler, Stalin, Machiavelli, Howard Hughes, Benedict Arnold, etc.

Think of someone you honor and list five characteristics of that person.

Person: _____

1.
2.
3.
4.
5.

Think of someone you dishonor (or think badly of) and list five characteristics of that person.

Person: _____

1.
2.
3.
4.
5.

Which person acts wisely? _____

Which person displays foolish characteristics? _____

Add these two verses to your charts (Prov. 3:34-35).

Questions to think about:

1. Describe the difference between grace and mercy and tell what they saved you from and to.

2. Are you a woman of honor or dishonor?

3. What do you need to begin to be aware of and to practice to make you more honorable?

4. Practice reciting your memorized verses.

My son …
For length …
Do not let …
So you will …
Trust in the _____ with all your _____
And do not _____ on your own _____
In all your _____ acknowledge Him,
And He will make your _____.

Week 4 / Day 3

Living Wisely

Hear, O sons, the instruction of a father,
And give attention that you may gain understanding.
For I give you sound teaching;
Do not abandon my instruction ....
Let your heart hold fast my words;
Keep my commandments and live.

PROVERBS *4:1-4*

Chapter four of Proverbs is again a treatise on wisdom. You will look at verses 1-13 today.

According to verse 5, what should you seek to own? _____

Vs. 6 What will wisdom do if you don't forsake her but, rather, love her? _____
_____

Vs. 7 What is the beginning of wisdom? _____

Will wisdom by itself be enough? _____

What else will you need? _____

Vs. 8 If I prize wisdom what will I get? _____

Vs. 8-9 If I embrace her what will I get? _____To be exalted means to be lifted up, to have a good reputation, to be honored.

According to vs. 10 what will it gain a son if he accepts these teachings from his father? _____
_____

Vs. 13 How is wisdom gained? _____

It sounds great, but now we need to make it practical. Review your memorized definition of wisdom. You will also see wisdom personified in a perfect form in Christ Jesus . Before you can gain wisdom (your memorized definition), you must get wisdom (Jesus Christ). Can an unbeliever be wise? (See 1 Cor.1 and 2.) _____

When you recognize Jesus as the Son of God and repent of your sins and decide to let Him be the Lord of your life, then you have begun your journey for wisdom. Matthew 6:33 reemphasizes this concept: "But seek _____His kingdom and His righteousness; and all these things shall be added to you."

What must you acquire first? _____

When we first obtain salvation and seek God's kingdom, then all the cares of the world (Matt. 6:25-32) will fall into place. Philippians 4:6 reminds you to "Be anxious for nothing, but in everything by prayer and supplication with thanksgiving let your requests be made known to God and the peace of God, which surpasses all comprehension, shall guard your hearts and minds in Christ Jesus."

Jesus will guard your heart and mind. Proverbs 4:6 promises you wisdom will guard you. What a mighty God we serve! If you do as Proverbs 3:6 says, "In all your ways acknowledge Him and He will make your paths straight." Put Jesus first (quiet times, obedience, prayer, good decisions based on God's Word, and the leading of the Holy Spirit), He will take care of the rest. He will exalt you, give you peace, honor you, give you long days, keep you from stumbling, and give you life. Does it sound like a journey you want to take? If Christ Jesus is your Savior and Lord, then hold on – keep on studying the Word and continue to grow daily in Him.

I decided to test God on His promise to guard my heart and my mind in Christ if I didn't worry. One of my children was in a tough place. He lived hundreds of miles from me, so I could not just drive to see him. Every time he came to mind (which was several times each day), I chose to give him to God. Praise God for him and his situation. I refused to worry and went on about my business. At first I would be back to worrying fairly quickly. As I practiced not worrying, but praying and praising, the easier it got to release him to God. And I walked in peace knowing his God cared for him, was watching over him, and was in control of the whole situation. God had guarded my mind.

Each situation I turn over to God and refuse to worry about brings calm and peace rather than worry and turmoil. What situation or person do you need to practice praying about and refuse to worry about? _____
_____

Does all of this mean Christians will never have bad things happen to them? Does it mean Christians will never be discouraged or sick? What about Romans 8:28? Turn to that verse now and read it. It says God will work all things to your good, not all things will be good. Christians get sick, die, get abused, and suffer depression. Jesus warned us that in this world we will face persecution and have troubles (Matthew 5:10, John 15:20). But Jesus also reminds us He will be with us always (Heb. 13:5). He gives us strength and joy in the midst of this earth's sorrows.

Don't forget to add these verses to your wisdom chart (Prov. 4:1-3).

Questions to think about:

1. If an unbeliever cannot be truly wise, then is wisdom more about your actions here on earth or your future in heaven?

2. Jesus gives you wisdom to live this life and to prepare for eternity. How can wisdom prepare you for eternity?

3. Do you tend to worry?

4. Is worry a sin?

5. What do you need to do when you are tempted to worry?

6. What is a worry concerning you right now you can give to God by thanking Him and asking Him to handle it?

7. Work on memorizing Proverbs 3:1-6.

    My son …
    For length …
    Do not let …
    So you will …

    Trust in the _____ with all your _____
    And do not _____ on your own _____.
    In all your _____ acknowledge Him,
    And He will make your _____.

Wisdom Found

> *Hear, my son, and accept my sayings*
> *And the years of your life will be many.*
> *I have directed you in the way of wisdom;*
> *I have led you in upright paths.*
> *When you walk, your steps will not be impeded;*
> *And if you run, you will not stumble.*
>
> PROVERBS 4:10-12

Break away from Proverbs and get a taste of the longest chapter in the Bible—Psalm 119.

Yesterday you learned that wisdom comes from instruction. Instruction is found in God's Word. The understanding you need comes through the Holy Spirit as you study God's Word.

Look up 1 Corinthian 2:12-14 and fill in the blanks.

"Now we have received, not the spirit of the _____, but the Spirit who is from _____, so we may know the things _____ given to us by God, which things we also speak, not in words taught by _____ wisdom, but those taught by the _____, combining spiritual thought with spiritual words."

Who is your teacher? _____

Without Jesus and the Holy Spirit, you can't understand, but because you have Jesus and the Spirit, you can learn the things of God. Ask Him to open your eyes of understanding and explain the Scriptures to you.

In the original Hebrew language Psalm 119 was done as an acrostic with each line beginning with a different Hebrew letter. Peruse chapter 119 and see if you can find words or phrases defining or explaining God's Word or your attitude towards it to complete the following acrostic.

Behold, I long for Your precepts (vs. 40).

I

B

L

E

G

O

D

'S

H

O

L

Y

W

O

R

D

The Psalmist had a lot to say about God's Word and its importance in your life. He used 176 verses to tell you about it.

Questions to think about:

1. What does following God's Word mean in your life?

2. What changes do you need to make so God's Word is a priority in each day?

3. Work on your memory verses.

My son …
For length …
Do not let …
So you will …
Trust in the _____ with all your _____
And do not _____ on your own _____.
In all your _____Him,
And He will _____ your _____.

Week 4 / Day 5

Worldviews

Do not enter the path of the wicked
And do not proceed in the way of evil men.
Avoid it, do not pass by it;
Turn away from it and pass on.

Proverbs 4:14-15

In contrast to Proverbs 4:1-13 where wisdom showed you her graces, verses 14-17 and verse 19 give you the picture of one who refuses this wisdom. First of all, recognize that going wisdom's way or the wicked way is a choice. Yes, your circumstances influence you, but you must take responsibility for your choices that lead day by day to the make-up of your life.

Verse 14 says,"Do not enter the path of the wicked
        And do not proceed in the way of evil men."

It sounds like a volitional choice. You can choose, therefore *Do Not!* This verse is an introduction to the second type of couplet found in Proverbs. It is a restatement. A line of instruction is given and to emphasize its importance, it is restated in the second line with different wording. In biblical writings, the more something is repeated, the more important it is.

The Bible writers did not have suffixes *-er* or *-est* to add to a word to show its comparative and superlative forms so words are repeated for emphasis.

What word is repeated in Isaiah 6:3? _____

What words are repeated in Revelation 19:16? _____

Here in Proverbs 4:14 the writer wants to get your attention. Hey! This is important!

Verse 15 is another restatement and gives further direction to verse 14:

> "Avoid it; do not pass by it;
> Turn away from it and pass on."

Notice in verse 14 that *wicked* is preceded by an article *the* making this word a noun. This is not just speaking of an evil deed here or there but following after wicked men and their ways. You will stumble and fall occasionally, but God's provision is 1 John 1:9—confession and forgiveness. (Don't forget: as God forgives you, forgive yourself also, and do Philippians 3:13-14).

Write what Philippians 3:13-14 tells you to do. _____

_____

_____

Proverbs 4:16-17 continues by telling you the consequences of a wicked life.

Be sure to add these to your foolishness charts in Appendix A.

It is interesting to note the wicked are not entirely without sleep. Apparently, after they have committed evil, they do sleep. Wickedness becomes like a drug or an intoxicating drink; they must continue to do wickedness in order to gain a few moments of sleep (see Prov. 4:17).

Proverbs 4:19 (you will study verse 18 tomorrow), tells you about the confusion, chaos, hopelessness and blindness of the wicked. They are so blind to wisdom, understanding, instruction, and spiritual insight they do not even know why they stumble. If you've ever tried to reason with a non-Christian who is far from God's calling, you will understand this. It is impossible to begin on the same page and so you will never agree on the final outcome.

Look back at verse 14 and notice this warning does not say not to earnestly go seeking evil or not to engross yourself in evil, but merely, "Do not enter the path," and "Do not proceed in the way." Stepping into a rampaging river can lead to your physical destruction; so it is spiritually: just stepping into that path—one drink, one drug, one lie, one cigarette—and you can be swept away into wickedness as a habit and a lifestyle. The best rule here is to flee temptation, and never give in to temptation to begin with.

This is a great time to study worldviews. A world view is a person's body of beliefs. For example, a Biblical Christian when asked, "Who are you?", might respond, "I am a created being made in the very image of God. I am His child." Whereas, someone who believes in evolution might reply, "I am a blob of tissue that came about by accident. There is no purpose or plan for my life. I get to decide how I live and die."

A world view answers eight questions. Write a brief answer to the following questions to summarize your world view. Remember to think big picture.

1. Who are we?
2. Where did we come from?
3. What does it mean to be human?
4. Why am I here?
5. What is wrong?
6. What is the solution? Is there a God?
7. Where are we going?
8. How can we get there?

Your answers to these questions define you as a Christian, a communist, a naturalist, an existentialist, etc. A great book to get you started in a world view study is *The Universe Next Door* by James W. Sire[13]. Check out C.S. Lewis' *Mere Christianity.*[14] Various titles by David Noebel are also very good. There are several good websites about worldviews.

Check out http://www.projectworldview.org/questions.html and worldviewacademy.com.

Add chapter 4:1-13 to your wisdom and foolishness charts.

Questions to think about:

1. How often must you choose to not enter the path of the wicked?

2. How can you avoid even entering the path of wickedness?

3. What influences do you have in your life you must guard against so you won't enter the path of wickedness?

4. Keep memorizing.

   My son …
   For length …
   Do not let …
   So you will …
   Trust in the _____ with all your _____
   And do not _____ on your own _____.
   In all your _____ Him,
   And He will make your _____.

5. Start adding Proverbs 3:7 to your memorized verses. Draw pictures in Appendix C.

Week 4 Group Discussion

1. Which life is more real—this earthly one or your eternal one? Explain. (Mark 2:5- 11, John 14:1-6, 17:3, Rev. 20:11-15, 21:1-7, 16-27, 22:1-6).

2. How are God's curses used to bless you? (Deut. 6, 8, 27, 28, 30:1-3, 15-20, 1 John 1:9).

3. Describe the difference between grace and mercy and tell what they saved you from and to. (Is. 63:8-9, Luke 1:77-79, Rom. 5:20-21, 9:15, 2 Cor. 12:9, Eph. 2:8, 2:4-7, Titus 3:7, Heb. 4:16, James 4:6).

4. If an unbeliever cannot be truly wise, then is wisdom more about your actions here on earth or your future in heaven? (1 Cor. 1:18-31, 2:1-16).

5. Jesus gives you wisdom to live this life and to prepare for eternity. How can wisdom prepare you for eternity? (1 Cor. 6:2-3).

6. What does following God's Word mean in your life? (Col. 3:16, 1 Thess. 2:13, 2 Tim. 3:16, James 1:21).

7. How often must you choose to not enter the path of the wicked? (Rom. 6:1-2, 11- 18, 13:14, 18:5-6).

8. How can you avoid even entering the path of wickedness? What influences do you have in your life you must guard against so you won't enter the path of wickedness?

9. Answer the worldview questions with biblical answers.

10. Is worry acceptable for a Christian or is it sin? (Prov. 3:5-6, Matt. 6:25, 6:34, Luke 12:25, Phil. 4:6-7, 1 Peter 5:6-7).

11. Recite Proverbs 3:1-6.

Guarding Your Heart

But the path of the righteous is like the light of dawn,
That shines brighter and brighter until the full day.

PROVERBS 4:18

Watch over your heart with all diligence,
For from it flow the springs of life.

PROVERBS 4:23

Proverbs 4:18 is such a contrast to where we left the evil person in yesterday's lesson. These verses are also your introduction to the third type of couplet—the enhancement. Line one will give its information and line two will follow by adding further information to it. These are often difficult to differentiate from the restatements; the clue is to look for additional information. In verse 18 line one reads, "But the path of the righteous is like the light of dawn." Line two adds, "That shines brighter and brighter until the full day."

What a difference from the darkness and hopelessness of Proverbs 4:17! The righteous sees his way and walks securely in it in front of all who might see and has always an upward hope that his way will be brighter and brighter (more clearly guided and seen) all the way until the full day (heaven).

Light and darkness cannot coexist. If you are a child of God with the Holy Spirit residing within you, then you cannot be possessed by demons. Where light is, darkness must flee. Demons can oppress a Christian. By shining God's light on your circumstances and your oppression, they, too, must flee.

Now you can begin to see clearly why this father (Solomon) writes with such earnestness to his son—not to put him down or keep him from having fun, but rather that he might taste the glorious light and not stumble along in the dark.

Read Proverbs 4:20-22 and add life and health to your wisdom chart in Appendix B.

To lead such a life is not easy and requires constant guarding. Read Proverbs 4:23: "_____ over your heart with all _____, for from it flows the springs of life."

How do you guard your heart? Write out 2 Corinthians 10:5: _____

_____

_____

_____

_____

Practice asking yourself a few questions about each thought or plan that comes into your mind until they become habit.

1. Is this thought pleasing unto the Lord?
2. Does this thought line up with what God says in Scripture?
3. Where is this thought originating??

Satan often puts thoughts into our minds, and being such a crafty fellow, he will put them in first person. For example, "I'm no good", "I'm just stupid", "I'm ugly". It is best to combat these with Scripture: "I am fearfully and wonderfully made". This is when using the truth of Scripture is so important. For further discussion on renewing your mind read Annabelle Gilliam's book, *The Confident Woman: Knowing Who You are in Christ.*[15]

Another way to guard your heart is being careful where and how you spend your time. A word on technology here. Technology is not good or evil, but rather, a tool. Make sure you are using it for God's glory and protecting yourself from evil influences with a filter, time boundaries, and prayer. A great book for helping you with this is *Biblically Handling Technology and Social Media: Applying Biblical Principles to Facebook, Texting, iPods, etc.* by Jobe Martin.[16]

Technology can become addictive. It changes the wiring of the brain. God created us so that work done in the executive center of the brain is wired to the pleasure center. We get pleasure from accomplishment. Technology skips the executive center of the brain and wires us straight through to the pleasure center. Immediate gratification without any effort. Who wouldn't want that! But the price is that our young people are not learning to function in the executive center where problem solving, organization, and planning happen.

One idea we utilized while the children were younger was coupons. They each got five ½ hour coupons a week for technology. They could use a coupon a day or save up and get 2½ hours on Saturday. They thought they were in charge, but we all know who really was in control!

Proverbs 4:24-27 continue the admonition of this loving parent.

Add verse 24 to your foolish chart Appendix A and verses 25-27 to your wisdom chart appendix B.

Notice again the diligence required in looking straight ahead, watching the path of your feet, and not turning to the right or left but keeping your feet from evil. Being single-focused on God and God's Word will result in a straight path. Singleness of focus in your studies, your work, your relationships, and your career decisions is also extremely important.

Deliberateness of purpose is also necessary when guarding your heart. "Archbishop Leighton said, 'To him that knoweth not the port to which he is bound, no wind is favorable. He may be well equipped, a good craft, sails set, ballast right, cargo well packed; but he wants somewhere to go, a port to enter. All his activity and preparation are useless without a purpose.'"[17]

The Apostle Paul shows singleness of purpose in Philippians 3:13-14. "But one thing I do …. I press on toward the goal for the prize of the upward call of God in Christ Jesus."

If you ask a gymnast where she looks and focuses as she walks the four-inch balance beam, you might expect her to reply, "My feet", but you will be surprised to find her focus is instead directed to the end of the beam. By watching that sturdy, nonmoving point to which she is headed, her feet find their stable places, one after another. Likewise, if you put your focus on Christ and direct your attention only to His desires and plans, you will be established, solid and permanent.

To neither turn to the right or left, one must first know the straight path. Where am I going? What activities, relationships, thoughts will get me there? Now, I do not believe God always shows you His whole plan for your life, but rather step by step He reveals His greater plan.

Write out Proverbs 16:9 _____

_____

Write out in the space below where you feel, and prayerfully have considered, is the direction God is leading you. Examples: to a daily quiet time, to a more respectful attitude toward siblings, to become a more motivated student or worker, to develop my skills with younger children, computers, etc.

Try to list at least 3.

1.
2.
3.

Questions to think about:

1. What thoughts has Satan put into your mind that you have chosen to believe?

2. How can you tell if a thought is your own, Satan's, or God's?

3. Explain Archbishop Leighton's quote and apply to your own life.

4. Work on your memorization of Proverbs 3:1-7.

    My son …
    For length …
    Do not let …
    So you will …
    Trust in the …
    And do not …
    In all your …
    And He will …

    Do not be _____ in your own _____,
    _____ the Lord and _____ from _____.

Week 5 / Day 2

The Pleasure of Sin

For the lips of an adulteress drip honey
And smoother than oil is her speech;
But in the end she is better as wormwood,
Sharp as a two-edged sword.
Her feet go down to death,
Her steps take hold of Sheol.
She does not ponder the path of life;
Her ways are unstable, she does not know it.

PROVERBS 5:3-6

Chapter 5 of Proverbs begins again with a plea, "Son, listen to me. I've been there, done that, or at least know others who have. Listen and learn." (My paraphrase). It is a lot easier to learn a moral lesson through observation rather than participation. Consequences are less this way. Listen to those who are older, respect their experiences, read books that have good examples of people who have chosen well and prospered, and of people who have chosen poorly and were led to destruction. Many famous artists, philosophers, musicians and politicians were successful in their careers, but because they followed after their own hearts, their lives ended in despair (Van Gogh, Voltaire, Rousseau, Degas, Hemmingway, etc.).

Look at Proverbs 5:3-6. The adulteress is that which leads one from his/her real Master and Creator. She is sin. In Hebrews you read about Moses who learned the lesson of saying *no* to sin and *yes* to eternal life even though sin was enticing.

Read Hebrews 11:25-26. "Choosing rather to endure ill-treatment with the people of God than to enjoy the
_____, considering the reproach
of Christ greater riches than the treasures of Egypt; for he was looking to the reward."

He was single-focused. Sin can be fun. It can feel good. It can fulfill for a short time. It is enticing. It offers popularity, acceptance, and friends. Sin looks good!

But look at Proverbs 5:4, "In the end she is as bitter as _____, Sharp as a two-edged sword." Verse 5 by saying that she leads to _____."

Sin, whether pride, disrespect, argumentativeness, bitterness, hate, anger, alcohol, drugs, murder, etc. leads eventually to destruction—destruction of relationships, of self-esteem, of dreams, of motivation, of life, etc.

Proverbs 5:9-14 describe what happens to one who continues in sin.

Add these to your chart in Appendix A.

Look up Romans 14:11, Philippians 2:10, and Isaiah 45:23-24. When sin entices you, what should you remember? _____

_____

You are God's sheep if you have believed that He is who He says He is and have chosen to trust in Him to make you a new creation. But, will you come into His kingdom with head bowed, bedraggled, and lame from sinful choices or will you leap joyously and with laughter when you see your Shepherd?

Take today's lesson time to go before God and ask Him to reveal to you any sin in your life. Be still before the Lord. If nothing comes to mind, spend time in praise and adoration for the forgiveness of your sins. If you are convicted of sin, be quick to confess and then remember to praise God for His mercy and grace.

Meditate on Psalm 51:6-13 and Isaiah 1:18.

Questions to think about:

1. When sin entices you what should you remember?

2. What sin do you have a tendency towards or had a tendency towards in the past?

3. How is it more rewarding to choose not to commit this sin rather to give in to it.

4. What are the rewards?

5. Work on memory verses Proverbs 3:1-7 and add verse 8 to your appendix C.

Contentment

Drink water from your own cistern
And fresh water from your own well …
Let your fountain be blessed,
And rejoice in the wife of your youth.

Proverbs 5:15, 18

Read Proverbs 5:15-23.

Solomon, the world's wisest man made some very bad choices, but he learned from them. This advice to his son was from experience. Solomon had 700 wives and 300 concubines! I can't even imagine. His wives were what pulled him away from God. (God had warned the Israelite kings not to multiply horses or wives—Deut. 17:14-17.)

Marriage is a sacred union between one man and one woman. You may be single, divorced, married, or married again. God's grace covers you. However, God does teach that the marriage bed is to be sacred. The relationship between husband and wife is to be pure. Finding contentment in whatever state you are in will bring peace and rest to your mind.

I remember hearing a report that said only 40% of couples who stay married past the first thirty years are ever truly happy.[18] I decided then that we would be one of those forty percenters. This took commitment in the first thirty years to stay and work things out. Divorce was not a word we ever used to threaten each other. Ruth Bell Graham, when asked if she ever considered divorcing Billy Graham, replied with humor, "Divorce never, homicide, yes!"[19] Many who have made it to those years beyond thirty, say marriage is even sweeter and more intimate and better than the first thirty years. I would agree.

Marriage does not depend on feelings of love. Love and marriage are commitments. There is no shame in asking for marriage advice or help from a more mature person in the church or a Christian counselor.

Proverbs 19:20 says, "Listen to _____ and accept _____,
That you may be wise the rest of your days."

And Proverbs 15:22 says, "Without consultation, plans are _____,
But with many counselors they succeed."

The three top reasons for divorce according to Christian counselor, Ellen Moore, is money, sex, and differences in disciplining children. The first two deal with our topic of covetousness. Handling money and learning to live within your means requires contentment in the present circumstances. Choosing to stay married means not coveting a different spouse, but rather learning to live with the one you have. Wandering eyes is the first step to adultery. Contentment at home is the answer to adultery.

If you are married, focus on that relationship. Marriage is really three relationships that must be balanced—a friendship (have fun together), a partnership (raising kids together, finances, yard work, etc.), and the romantic intimacy relationship. Most marriages do well in two areas and struggle in the third. Which two are you good at? _____

Which one do you need to work on? _____

And remember, Ladies, your man doesn't read your mind. Be sure to work on communicating and listening skills. (My four top books on marriage are: *His Needs/Her Needs* by William Harley,[20] *Cracking the Communication Code* by Emerson Eggerichs,[21] *Love & Respect* by Emerson Eggerichs,[22] and *The Five Love Languages* by Gary Chapman.[23])

Singles, God has a plan for your life. Jumping from bed to bed, man to man, will only bring great guilt, and possibly sickness or an unwanted pregnancy. When you are having sex, phenyl ethylamine (PEA) is involved. This chemical which is also present in cocoa and chocolate elevates energy, mood and attention. PEA is produced in greater amounts when one is in love; conversely a deficiency causes unhappy feelings. The first time you have sex, bonding occurs by rising PEA, oxytocin and dopamine levels at a level greater than any other time. This continues for about a year. That is why the first year of marriage is called the Honeymoon Period.[24] If you have slept with others before marriage, then you won't get that surge of chemicals to carry you through. You will feel less and less satisfied with each sexual encounter. If you are not a virgin, confess this to God, repent, and walk forward clean and without guilt.

I Corinthians 7:3 does say a husband and a wife have a duty to one another for sex. I struggled with this for a long time due to sexual abuse in my childhood, but finally decided if sex was my duty, I would enjoy it! Duty became a treat. That is why Proverbs 5:18 says, "And rejoice in the wife [or husband] of your _____."

Even though Proverbs 5:15-23 is dealing with faithfulness within marriage, these verses lead to a greater discussion on contentment. Contentment springs from a grateful heart. When you are satisfied and thankful for what you have, you rejoice and are fulfilled. When you begin comparing that which you have to what others have you become unsatisfied and get the wants. If you compare, you will despair!

This sin can be coveting someone besides your mate, as in the Proverbs, but it also includes covetousness of clothes, cars, careers, children, relationships, houses, positions, etc.

List things you tend to covet.

1.
2.
3.
4.
5.

My husband and I have agreed to help each other with this by not looking a catalogs or circulars that come in the mail. We also do not spend our time at the mall or window shopping unless we have something specific in mind. Sticking to our grocery list at stores and seeking permission from one another before impulse buying over $20 helps us to have some accountability in our finances. When we get the wants, we remind each other of all God's blessings, what we do have, and the choices we have made that limit financial income such as homeschooling and being in ministry, and we realize these choices are more important than "stuff".

What are some steps you can take to flee from temptation?

1.
2.
3.
4.
5.

Try to list 20 things for which you are grateful to God.

You might post this on your refrigerator door!

Lastly, Proverbs 5:21 should help you keep within moral boundaries. "For the ways of _____ are before the eyes of the _____, and He watches all his paths."

Nothing you do or dwell on is hidden from God, and all will be revealed in the end.

Read Psalm 139:1-6.

Verses 1-3 include all of your activity. Verse 4 includes your thoughts. Verse 5 shows Gods omnipresence. These verses should not scare the child of God, but rather comfort him. It's okay if a great and wonderful, loving and forgiving Father knows everything about you—He's safe, because He hides you under His wings and His love is so everlasting. Live within that knowledge and take comfort from the fact He cares that much for you. Remember an ounce of prevention is worth a pound of cure. Yes, God's grace extends to those times you mess up, but it is so much better if you obey and stay within His arms of protection.

Add Proverbs 5:22-23 to your foolishness chart in Appendix A.

10 Things to Do to Experience Contentment and Joy in the Midst

1. **Go to God.** – Psalm 94:19-20: "When my anxious thoughts multiply within me, Your consolations delight my soul."
   Psalm 43:4: "Then I will go to the alter of God, to God my exceeding joy."

2. **Know God's heart.** – Ian Macleron said, "Those who know the path to God can find it in the dark."

3. **Trust God.** – "When you can't see God's hand, trust His heart."–Spurgeon
   Proverbs 3:5-6: "Trust in the Lord with all your heart and do not lean on your own understanding. In all your ways acknowledge Him, and He will make your paths straight."

4. **Obey God.** – John 15:10-11: "If you keep My commandments, you will abide in My love; just as I have kept My Father's commandments and abide in His love. These things I have spoken to you so that My joy may be in you, and that your joy may be made full."

5. **Listen for God's voice.** – John 3:29: "He who has the bride is the bridegroom; but the friend of the bridegroom, who stands and hears him, rejoices greatly because of the bridegroom's voice. So this joy of mine has been made full."

6. **Worship God.** – Luke 24:52: "And they, after worshiping Him, returned to Jerusalem with great joy."

7. **Abide in the word, in God, in Christ.** –John 15:5: "I am the vine, you are the branches; he who abides I Me and I in him, he bears much fruit, for apart from Me you can do nothing."

8. **Recognize God's power.** — Luke 10:17: "The seventy returned with joy, saying, 'Lord, even the demons are subject to us in Your name.'"

9. **Think on these things.** — Philippians 4:8: "Finally, brethren, whatever is true, whatever is honorable, whatever is right, whatever is pure, whatever is lovely, whatever is of good repute, if there is any excellence and if anything worthy of praise, dwell on these things."

10. **Do what brings you joy.** — Psalm 37:4: "Delight yourself in the Lord, and He will give you the desires of your heart." He puts His desires within us, so we should celebrate by following them!

Questions to think about:

1. Are you content in your present relationship status?

2. What commitment or renewal of a commitment do you need to make?

3. What type of things do you covet?

4. Were you able to come up with 20 things you are grateful for?

5. Practice reciting Proverbs 3:1-8.

> My son …
> For length …
> Do not let …
> So you will …
> Trust in the …
> And do not …
> In all your …
> And He will …

> Do not be _____ in your own _____,
> _____ the Lord and _____ from _____ .
> It will be _____ to your body And _____ to
> your bones.

Surety and Pledges

My son, if you have become surety for your neighbor …
If you have been snared with the words of your mouth …
Go, humble yourself, and importune your neighbor.

PROVERBS 6:1, 2, 3

$\mathcal{R}$ead Proverbs 6:1-5. Here are some explanations that may help.

"Have become surety for your neighbor" means, "One who is bound with and for another who is primarily liable, and who is called the principal; one who engages to answer for another's appearance in court, or for his payment of a debt.[25]

"Have given a pledge for a stranger" means having vouched for someone's character who you really don't know.

"Being snared with the words of your mouth" and "Have been caught with the words of your mouth"—this could be a lie, a half-truth (at our house a half-truth is a whole lie), gossip, outbursts of anger, disputes, foul language, etc.

Read James 3:2-12.
Have you been guilty of sins of the tongue? _____

Read Proverbs 6:3-5 and repent!

This requires humbling yourself to go and confess and to importune (urge, or entreat persistently) your neighbor. You are not to do this tomorrow, but do it now before the sun has set. This confession is likened to releasing a gazelle from the hunter's hand or a bird from the hand of the fowler. Asking forgiveness or confronting a misunderstanding takes courage and humility, but will reap peace and joy. Write out Romans 12:18: _____

_____

_____

Now, a hunter is dangerous to a gazelle, and a fowler is dangerous to a bird thus, surety, pledges, and the words of your mouth can be dangerous to your soul. It is urgent you be released from such actions. This passage should also reveal to you that pledges and sureties are wrong to begin with. Mom and Dad, don't cosign for a car for your teenager. Let them take on their own responsibilities and face the good or bad consequences of their actions. This leads to further responsibility and the ability to try new things and self-respect.

The answer to disengaging yourself from any mess you have caused due to surety, a pledge, or the words of your mouth is to humble yourself and go to your neighbor in repentance. We all hate the feeling of having to humble ourselves to one another. It is hard, but still easier to humble ourselves before a holy God than it is to humble ourselves to one another. Why is this? Humility requires you to put your pride behind you. If your self-esteem is built upon what others think about you or how well you accomplish tasks, then humility is a real hit to the ego. If your self-esteem is built on the fact you are God's child, a sinner saved by grace, then it is easier to go humbly to another. Realizing you are not perfect and neither is anyone else can make humbling yourself easier.

Because I know how hard it is to humble myself before another with a confession of sin, I will offer more grace when someone comes to me with repentance. Humility can mend friendships and allow you to develop deeper relationships. The feeling of relief makes being humble well worth it.

Add drawings in Appendix C from Proverbs 3:9-10 and start memorizing.

Questions to think about:

1. Why, do you think, God is against surety?

2. How is a half-truth a whole lie?

3. What sins of the tongue do you struggle with?

4. Why does it seem easier to ask for God's forgiveness than man's?

5. What do you base your self-esteem on—how you look, what you do, others' opinions about you, or that you are God's beloved child?

6. Recite to someone Proverbs 3:1-8.
   Here's some clues for your two newest verses: 7 and 8.

   Do not be _____ in your own _____ ,
   _____ the Lord and _____ from _____ .
   It will be _____ to your body
   And _____ to your bones.

Industry vs. Idleness

Go to the ant, O sluggard,
Observe her ways and be wise.

PROVERBS 6:6

ead Proverbs 6:6-11.

For a moment, stop and think about the ant. According to the Smithsonian website[26], there are more ants than any other insect on earth. They are found all over the world except the extreme North and South poles. Ants are ever busy in the warmer months but hibernate during the winter months, therefore they must collect enough food during the warmer seasons to allow them to hibernate without starving. Ants can carry loads many times heavier than themselves, whether they are harvester ants–cutting and collecting seeds; or honey ants – collecting juices from flowers; or "cow-keeping" ants–keeping aphids, leafhoppers and certain caterpillars as pets and collect the honeydew they drop from their abdomens; or slave-making ants capturing another species of ants to do the hard labor; or even army ants going on hunting expeditions for insects and small animals. Find a drawing of an ant from an encyclopedia or nature book and draw it here as you meditate on the ants' productivity and wisdom. Stick drawings and cartoons are fine.

Ants are constantly on the go and busy. They are industrious. As the author of Proverbs records, "Go to the ant, O sluggard, observe her ways and be wise, which having no chief, officer, or ruler, prepares her food in the summer and gathers her provision in harvest."

"Idleness" according to William Thayer in his book, *Gaining Favor with God and Man*, "is the mother of poverty, vice, and crime, having a family too numerous to be counted."[27]

When Romans, generals and statesmen, tilled the soil of Italy, the Roman Empire flourished. When slaves were introduced and labor became discreditable to those who could live without it, the ruling class gave itself to pleasure and luxury; soon corruption was everywhere and the empire fell.

Even Adam was required to labor in the Garden of Eden by His creator—and this before sin entered the world (Gen. 2:15). Work, or labor, the very ability to accomplish work, is a gift of God. "Idle hands are the devil's workshop," has proven true throughout history. Inner city gangs are a result of such idleness by older teens and younger adults who have not been taught to put their energies towards worthwhile ventures.

Read Proverbs 6:9-11.

What will, "A little sleep, a little slumber, a little folding of the hands to rest," lead to? _____

List the work God would have you to do. Work may include an occupation, taking care of children, ministry, yard work, house work, volunteer work, etc.

Remember, though, the work of a Christian is not busyness for the kingdom, but rather prayer first, then obedience. 1 Corinthians 3:11-15 explains that works done through obedience will pass through fire unharmed, but works done for selfish motives or selfish ambition will burn up.

> "According to the grace of God which was given to me, like a wise master builder I laid a foundation, and another is building on it. But each man must be careful how he builds on it. For no man can lay a foundation other than the one which is laid, which is Jesus Christ. Now if any man builds on the foundation with gold, silver, precious stones, wood, hay, straw, each man's work _____
> _____; for the day will show it because it is to be revealed with fire, and the fire itself will test the _____ of each man's work. If any man's work which he has built on it remains, he will receive a reward. If any man's work is burned up, he will suffer loss; but he himself will be saved, yet so as ____
> _____."

How will your life's work stand the test of fire? Are you working for approval or working out of obedience?
_____ _____ _____

Questions to think about:

1. Why is work good for your physical health? Your mental health? Your emotional health?

2. What type of work do you like to do best?

3. Fill in the blanks for Proverbs 3:1-8.

My son, do not _____ my _____,
But let your _____ keep my _____;
For _____ of _____ and _____ of _____
And _____ they will _____ to you.
Do not let _____ and _____ leave you;
_____ them around your neck,
_____ them on the _____ of your_____,
So you will find _____ and good _____
In the _____ of _____ and _____.
_____ in the _____ with all _____.
And do not _____ on you own _____,
In _____ your ways _____ Him,
And He will make your _____.
Do not be _____ in your own eyes;
Fear the _____ and _____ away from evil.
It will be _____ to your body
And _____ to your bones.

Week 5 Group Discussion

1. What lies has Satan put into your mind that you have chosen to believe? (John 8:44, Rom. 1:25, 2 Cor. 10:3-5).

2. When you recognize a lie you have been believing, how can you combat it? (Matt. 4:4, 7, 10, 2 Cor. 10:5. You do this by finding a truth in God's word and speaking this truth against Satan.)

3. Explain Archbishop Leighton's quote and apply to your own life. ("To him that knoweth not the port to which he is bound, no wind is favorable. He may be well equipped, a good craft, sails set, ballast right, cargo well packed; but he wants somewhere to go, a port to enter. All his activity and preparation are useless without a purpose."[28] (Heb. 6:19, 10:23, 1 Cor. 9:24-27).

4. When sin entices you what should you remember? (John 14:6, Rom. 3:23, Col.3:6-15, John 2:1, 2:16, 2:21, 2:28, 3:4-8, 4:4).

5. How is it more rewarding to choose not to commit this sin rather to give in to it. What are the rewards? (Renewed relationship with God the Father, strengthening of your discerning of the Holy Spirit's conviction, no guilt feelings, confidence before God, and a pure and sincere heart–John 15:10-11, 1 John 3:21).

6. What type of things do you covet? (Luke 3:14, 2 Cor. 12:10, Phil. 4:11, Heb. 13:5, James 4:1-3).

7. How can you remember your blessings and why is this important? (Eph. 1:3-8, James 1:17).

8. How is a half-truth a whole lie? (1 John 2:21).

9. Recite aloud Proverbs 3:1-8.

10. Share drawings from day 4.

Week 6 / Day 1

Foolish Behaviors

These are six things which the Lord hates,
Yes, seven which are an abomination to Him.

PROVERBS 6:16

$\mathcal{G}$et your pen ready to add to your foolish chart. (Appendix A) This is pretty specific. Read Proverbs 6:12-19

Verse 12 – A perverse mouth is a characteristic of foolishness. The result is a worthless person and a wicked man.

Verse 13 – Winking of the eye, signaling with the foot, and pointing with the fingers are characteristics of foolishness.

Verse 14 – A foolish person devises evil, has a perverse heart, and spreads strife.

Verse 15 – The result of all this foolishness is that calamity will come suddenly; instantly he will be broken; there will be no healing.

Verse16 – God hates these things; they are an abomination to Him.

Verse 17-19 – Characteristics of a fool:

1. Haughty eyes
2. Lying tongue
3. Hands that shed innocent blood

4. Heart that devises wicked plans
5. Feet that run rapidly to evil
6. A false witness who utters lies
7. One who spreads strife among brothers

Ouch! I know we are all guilty of at least one or perhaps two or three of these.

Add them to your chart and go back and look at them closer.

The first thing you will notice is of these 14 abominations, five have to do with your tongue—your words. God says a wicked man has a perverse mouth. The literal meaning of *perverse* is "Directed away from what is right or good; obstinately persisting in an error or fault."[29]

Notice again, good or evil is a choice. Proverbs 18:21says, "Death and life are in the power of the tongue, and those who love it will eat its fruit." Your words can bring life to a person through praise, truth, teaching, etc, or your words can be perverse and bring death. A perverse tongue might include gossip, cursing, cussing, negative criticism, continual belittling, lying, sneering, making fun of, sarcasm, etc. You may be able to add others.

Spreading strife is mentioned twice in this section. First as a general statement, then as a more specific statement—spreading strife among brothers (this includes sisters, too). This is especially loathsome to your God because of the high value God puts upon families. He created families to be a support system, a safe place, a haven from the world. When strife is spread among brothers, there is no place one can be at ease, at rest, comforted. I believe we can also stretch this in New Testament times to the brotherhood of Christians. The world is to know you are a Christian by your love for others in the Church. If someone is spreading strife in the family of God, then the Church will lose its witness. Our difference lies in the fact that we love one another. This is what will draw the world to investigate Jesus. Don't be part of the problem—watch your tongue. (See Francis Schaeffer's book, *The Mark of a Christian*.[30])

Continuing with the tongue's evils, you will notice the next one listed is lying. This, of course, includes the out and out falsehood, but I would suggest it covers much more. At our house, "Half a truth is a whole lie." Boy, that can trip you up! Leading someone to believe something false by your silence is a lie. It really is a question of your heart—if you set out to deceive, it's a lie.

Proverbs 6:13 always brings with it an interesting discussion. Winking of the eye, signaling with the foot, and pointing with the fingers are all acts of conniving. These are usually done behind your victim's back. Usually the victim is the butt of a joke, unkind remark, or prank. God would rather you not say or do anything you can't do in front of someone else.

Haughty eyes is a sin which will catch many a man or woman. Rolling of your eyes when you don't agree or think someone doesn't know what they are talking about is nothing but haughtiness—pride. It's a good thing to catch this prideful action and practice not rolling your eyes, but rather throw up a prayer of thankfulness for the one in your life who sometimes frustrates you.

"Hands that shed innocent blood" includes, but is not limited to murder, abortion, infanticide, and euthanasia. It would include the person who encouraged another to perform any of these acts as well. The sin is in the heart, not just in the actual action.

It all comes from the heart. A heart that devises wicked plans or devises evil will manifest itself through the words and actions of the fool. Write out 2 Corinthians 10:5. _____

_____

_____

This verse needs to apply to the words of our mouth as well as the intentions of our heart and our thoughts. Romans 12:2 says, "And do not be conformed to this world, but be transformed by the renewing of your mind, so that you may prove what the will of God is, that which is good and acceptable and perfect." As you become "transformed by the renewing of your mind," your words and actions will come under the command of the Holy Spirit and will be transformed as well.

Put a star by any of the following foolish actions you sometimes get caught doing. Begin to pray now that God will help you catch yourself the next time you do this and choose to repent and give a blessing instead.

gossip   cursing   cussing   criticism   belittling   lying

sneering   making fun   spreading strife   winking of the eye

signaling with the feet   pointing with the fingers (literally or in your mind)

haughty eyes

Questions to think about:

1. Are your words to others bringing life or death?

2. How is half a truth a whole lie?

3. Which of these sins has become a habit for you?

4. Are you going to commit to not doing that which is an abomination to God?

5. Add Proverbs 5:9 and 10 to your Appendix C.

𝒟iscipline vs. 𝒫unishment

For the commandment is a lamp and the teaching is light;
And reproofs for discipline are the way of life
To keep you from the evil woman,
From the smooth tongue of the adulteress.

PROVERBS 6:23-24

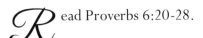ead Proverbs 6:20-28.

Focus today on discipline–God's discipline. Your memory work of Proverbs 3 includes these lines, "Do not reject the discipline of the Lord, nor loathe His reproof, for whom the Lord loves He reproves, even as a father corrects the son in whom he delights" (Prov. 3:11-12).

The only commandment with a promise is "Honor your father and mother, as the Lord your God has commanded you that your days may be prolonged, and that it may go well with you in the land which the Lord God gives you" (Deut. 5:16). (More on honoring parents–whether they are honorable or not in Practical Proverbs for Women Book 2.) We are to honor others as well.

Proverbs 6:20 is a practical step in honoring. Time to check your heart. When you are pulled over by a policeman for speeding or reprimanded at work for a failure or misstep or your spouse points out an error or habit do you harbor resentment, wallow in bitterness, or are you quick to repent and quick to reconcile? _____

Remember discipline does not just refer to punishment but also includes teaching of those habits which will lead one to a full and healthy life. Discipline is designed to teach a better way, whereas punishment aims at stopping a specific behavior.

My husband often comforted me after a long day of reminders to our five boys saying, "God gave them to us for 18-20 years because He knew we would have to say the same things every day for that whole time for them to finally get it." It's not nagging–it's training!

2 Timothy 3:16 reminds you that the Bible is the instruction manual for life and is profitable for what four things?

1.
2.
3.
4.

One more word on the benefits of discipline. Look at 2 Timothy 2:3-6. What three careers are compared to your Christian walk?

1.
2.
3.

You are a soldier of Christ and need to be about disciplining yourself to the rigors of military life. You are in a race and need to be disciplined so you might run to win, and, as a farmer, who has been disciplined in his labors and will reap the benefits of his hard work, so you who labor diligently will reap eternal life with Christ Jesus your Lord.

Those who have been reared by discipline learn to respect and be grateful for the rules, boundaries, and confines. On the other hand, if one has not bent their knee to discipline's molding power, he finds himself fighting discipline as if it were the enemy–taking away his rights of freedom of choice and freedom of speech. An undisciplined person will eventually come to loathe any and all authority placed over him including the loving, caring, faithful Creator God.

At that point, Proverbs 6:24-28 becomes reality. These verses compare the consequences of not being disciplined to giving in to the evil woman. She personifies pride, selfishness, and all the sins that come from a heart dripping with evil. Write verse 27 here: _____

_____

_____

What is your answer to this question? _____

Can a man ignore discipline and not suffer the bad consequences? _____

Questions to think about:

1. How is being a Christian like a soldier?

2. How is being a Christian like an athlete?

3. How is being a Christian like a farmer?

4. Which of these metaphors challenges you the most?

5. Recite Proverbs 3:1-10 aloud.

My son, do not _____ my _____,
But let your _____ keep my _____;
For _____ of _____ and _____ of _____
And _____ they will _____ to you.
Do not let _____ and _____ leave you;
_____ them around your neck,
_____ them on the _____ of your _____,
So you will find _____ and good _____
In the _____ of _____ and _____.
_____ in the _____ with all _____.
And do not _____ on you own _____,
In _____ your ways _____ Him,
And He will make your _____.
Do not be _____ in your own eyes;
Fear the _____ and _____ away from evil.
It will be _____ to your body
And _____ to your bones.
Honor the Lord from your _____
And from the first of all your _____;
So your barns will be filled with _____
And your vats will overflow with _____.

Lust, Sin, Death

For the ways of a man are before the eyes of the Lord,
And He watches all his paths.
His own iniquities will capture the wicked,
And he will be held with the cords of his sin.
He will die for lack of instruction,
And in the greatness of his folly he will go astray.

PROVERBS 5:21-23

Discipline, you learned yesterday, is a safeguard. If you succumb to biblical discipline, you also reap the benefits of biblical living. Proverbs 6:24-28 tells you what the result is of denying or turning away from discipline. Remember in the Old Testament, adultery is often the imagery used for all things pulling you away from God (including but not limited to a sexual affair).

In Proverbs 6:25 where does the lie begin? _____ (Quick note: even though Proverbs seems to be talking to men only, don't forget, sisters, you too can fall into the same traps and troubles, for you are a part of mankind.) So sin begins in your heart. Your heart is the doorway of choice. Even Jesus was tempted. It is not sinful to be tempted or to have a tempting thought. What you do with temptation or thoughts leads you to sin or righteousness.

James 1:14-15 holds the key. Write these verses out here. _____
_____
_____
_____
_____

This is the LSD principle. Lust leads to sin which leads to death.

L – lust
S – sin
D – death

Where is the beginning of lust? Lust is the deep desire or longing for something. Lust can be sexual, but can also be food, acceptance, a bigger house, etc. Lust begins as jealousy and becomes envy until finally turning into lust demanding action.

Turn to 1 John 2:15-16 and fill in the blanks.

"Do not love the _____ nor the things in the _____.
If anyone loves the _____, the love of the Father is not in him. For all that is in the _____, the lust of the _____ and the lust of the _____ and the boastful _____ of life, is not from the Father, but is from the _____."

You are tempted by what you see, what you desire, what you think will fulfill and bring power. But you are to be in the world, but not of the world (John 15:19).

1 John 2:17 goes on to state, "The _____ is passing away, also its _____; but the one who does the will of God lives forever."

Once again there are choices: temporary fulfillment vs. eternal glory with Christ. The absolute necessity of hiding God's Word in your heart to keep from sinning and to be transformed by the renewing of your mind is foundational to holy living and peace.

Many godly people fall away from biblical principles due to sexual sin. Safeguard your life by not having a friend of the opposite sex (unless you and your husband are friends with the husband and wife and only do things as a foursome). Don't go looking for trouble by flirting. If you are having sexual fantasies of someone beside your spouse, remove yourself from that person's life. Pornography is an emotional affair. Marriage will not thrive with one partner viewing pornography. Inappropriate sexual thoughts may come into your mind. Keep your thoughts under control, pray, discipline yourself to think on the things mentioned in Philippians 4:8.

According to this verse what should you focus on? Things that are ...

1.
2.
3.

4.

5.

6.

7.

8.

Then again, there's always ice cream! When we were questioning one of our boys about how he handles the visual desires when he sees young women scantily dressed, he replied that he thinks about ice cream. It's right, pure, lovely, excellent and worthy of praise! I think God meant to think upon the Words of Scripture, but if ice cream works, go for it! Either way, be quick to forgive yourself, refocus, and most importantly, "Now flee from youthful _____ and pursue righteousness, faith, love and peace, with those who call on the Lord from a pure heart"
(2 Timothy 2:22).

If going to the beach and seeing others in swimsuits brings about thoughts of sex, then don't go to the beach. If the internet poses enticing views, stay offline or get a filter. Know that by disciplining yourself, you will find so much more pleasure, ease, and joy in your life partner's arms. If you succumb to even dwell on such thoughts they will lead to sin (even sinful attitudes) as Proverbs 6:26-28 state they, "Will reduce you to a loaf of bread, burn you and scorch you."

Questions to think about:

1. Try to not think of the number 7.

2. Seven is probably all you can think about. Now think about the number 21. Are thinking about 7 anymore?

3. Your mind can only think on one thing at a time. When you are tempted by the things of this world, what verse of Scripture can you meditate on to keep your mind focused on God.

4. Practice your memory verses through vs. 10.

> My son …
> But let your …
> For …
> And …
> Do not let …
> Bind …
> Write …
> So you will …
> In the …

Trust ...
And do not ...
In all ...
And He ...
Do not be ...
Fear ...
It will be ...
And honor the Lord from your _____
And from the first of all your _____;
So your barns will be filled with _____
And your vats will overflow with _____.

Week 6 / Day 4

Leaving Sin Behind

*My son, keep my words
And treasure my commandments within you.
Keep my commandments and live,
And my teaching as the apple of your eye.*

PROVERBS 7:1-2

Read all of Proverbs chapter 7 noting the characteristics (enticements) of sin and the results of sin. Add to chart Appendix A.

First John has a lot to relate to you about sin. First of all, if someone had never committed a sinful deed or broken a rule (impossible in your flesh or own desires), he would still be a sinner because he inherited a sin nature from Adam. If you ever doubt this inherited sin, just watch a two-year-old. No one had to teach him to stomp his foot or turn away from his mother's voice or do what he wishes in spite of parental direction. He has to be trained in righteousness to learn what *no* means.

In our house, *no* meant, "It's not going to happen so quit asking." Having a three or four-year-old repeat back the meaning of "no" when he wants to throw a fit or argue tends to stop him in his tracks!

1 John 1:8 says "If we say we have _____, we are deceiving ourselves, and the _____ is not in us."

As a Christian, your sin nature is replaced by God's Holy Spirit. You are "A new creature, behold old things are passed away" (2 Cor. 5:17). The power of the Holy Spirit is upon you to convict you of your sin. However, because you continue to live in a sinful body and in a sinful world, the option is always there to choose to commit acts of sins even though you've been cleansed from the inherited sin.

Thus 1 John 1:9 says, "If we confess _____, He is faithful and righteous to forgive us our sins and cleanse us from all unrighteousness."

Even Paul dealt with sin. In Romans 7:14-8:6, he knew and experienced the war we must all face. He knew what was right to do, but failed to do it. Read this passage.

Romans 8:1 is a great verse to memorize. "Therefore there is now _____ _____ for those who are in Christ Jesus."

This is a good thing. This is a statement of your position in Christ, not about your conduct. You are held accountable for the sinful deeds or attitudes you have as a born again Christian, but sin does not change your position as God's beloved child, redeemed and bought with a forever price. One might ask, "Then, if I am born again, can I go on sinning?" The answer to this is found in Romans 6:1-2. "What shall we say then? Are we to continue in sin so that grace may increase? May it never be! How shall we who died to sin still live in it?"

There are several reasons Christians should leave their sin behind them.

1. Christ died for you. Out of sheer gratitude you should live to please Him.

2. Sin separates you relationally from God.

3. Sins carry with them dire consequences which are not befitting a son or daughter of the King.

4. The laws are put into place for your protection and provision. By following them you will find happiness and great joy.

5. As you strive towards holiness, knowing you cannot attain it without God, you grow in your relationship with God.

6. Others are watching you. You don't want to give them an excuse not to become a Christian.

7. The fruit of the Holy Spirit cannot grow within you if your roots are not planted deep in the word and arms outstretched to God's goodness.

8. If you are praying and praising God and desiring to live with Him, the Holy Spirit will convict you of your sin, and you will be most miserable.

The key is to live and walk and abide in the Spirit, to be studying the Word of God, memorizing the Word of God, meditating upon the Word, being in a constant state of prayer and communication with your Father in heaven, and choosing to put aside the things of this world. That's a big order!

You don't have to join a convent or become a hermit; there is a balance. A biblical life can be led in America in the 21ˢᵗ century, but it is challenging and requires constant watch, minute by minute choices, and the assurance and hope of Christ. My husband has often said that he felt like a fish swimming upstream as we made unpopular choices such as my staying home to raise the children rather than becoming a career woman; homeschooling; monitoring television, movies, music, friends, and activities; not allowing our children to stay for extended amounts of time with relatives due to lifestyle differences; and even moving as the Lord opened up to us new avenues of ministry. But these sacrifices have been worth it all. God has blessed all five boys with hearts ready and wanting to serve Him. They are making wise choices and desiring to live lives worthy of Christ's sacrifice. What more could a parent hope for?

Of course, they are human; they make mistakes, they sin, and they frustrate me with their immaturity at times, but they are quick to repent and striving towards maturity. Parenting is about the relationship. They are my sons. Period. Even when they mess up, I love them. Psalm 37:23-24 sums up God's relationship of love with us. Take another look at this verse: "And He delights in his (man's) way. When he falls, he will not be hurled headlong, because the Lord is the one who holds his hand." Notice that this does not say that "if" he falls, but rather "when" He falls. God knows we are not perfect. He knows our frame is mindful that we are but dust and loves us anyway (Psalm 103:13)!

You are God's delight! I imagine a father teaching his son to walk. When the child falls down, Dad is not there with a lecture and a frown or disappointment. No, rather, he picks the child up with a giggle and a tickle, sets him back on his feet and lets him try again within the reach of the father's protective embrace.

What nature has God redeemed in you? _____

Does that mean you will never sin again? _____

When you do mess up, what are you to do? _____

Remember, "There is therefore now no condemnation for those who are in Christ Jesus." Be quick to repent and strive towards holy living.

There is a difference between confession and repentance. Confession is admitting you are guilty. Repentance is turning from an action never to do it again (Rom. 6:11-13). 1 John 1:9 requires confession. Confession cleanses you for the moment and renews your relationship with God until you repeat that or another offense. But repentance is a heart change. If someone hurts me badly due to sin, I want to see true repentance before I get close to them again.

Think about a caterpillar which has become a butterfly. This creature can now fly. How sad if you see it walking along the ground trying to find its way. As a born again Christians, you are that butterfly. You can fly and soar above life's circumstances. You have the ability, but how sad it is to be crawling around absorbed in the grass of life instead of flying through the skies. This is what happens when you choose, as a Christian, to sin. You have the power not to sin (Rom. 6:6-7), but you probably don't always use this ability. Make sure you are living life on an eagle's wing, high above the sin and garbage of this world.

Questions to think about:

1. If you are born again, you are no longer a caterpillar, but a butterfly. Are you soaring in the clouds or still trying to get up off the ground?

2. Why should you who are forgiven from your sins, no longer live in sin?

3. God is like a father, only perfect. This makes you His son or daughter. How does God respond to His children's sin?

4. Say your memory verses Proverbs 3:1-10.

      My son …
      But let your …
      For …
      And …
      Do not let …
      Bind …
      Write …
      So you will …
      In the …
      Trust …
      And do not …
      In all …
      And He …
      Do not be …
      Fear …
      It will be …
      And …
      Honor the _____ from your _____
      And from the _____ of all your _____;
      So your _____ will be filled with _____
      And your _____ will overflow with _____.

Week 6 / Day 5

Who is Wisdom?

I, wisdom, dwell with prudence,
And I find knowledge and discretion ...
Counsel is mine and sound wisdom;
I am understanding, power is mine.

Proverbs 8:12, 14

Chapter 8 of Proverbs is really a riddle and a very foundational one at that. Here are some of the clues:

8:1   Does not wisdom call?

8:7   For my mouth will utter truth; and wickedness is an abomination to my lips.

8:11   Wisdom is better than jewels and all desirable things cannot compare with her.

8:17   And those who diligently seek me will find me.

8:22   The Lord possessed me at the beginning of His way before His works of old.

8:27   When He established the heavens, I was there.

8:30   Then I was beside Him as a master workman.

8:32   For blessed are they who keep my ways.

8:35   For he who finds me finds life and obtains favor from God.

Who is wisdom? _____Still not sure?

Narrow it down. Look at:

8:32	Wisdom is the Way
8:7	Wisdom is Truth
8:35	Wisdom is life

Sound familiar? Try John 14:6, "_____ said to him, 'I am the Way, the Truth, and the Life; no one comes to the Father but through Me.'"

That's right, Jesus is the personification of wisdom. I Corinthians 1:24 states that Christ is the power of God and the wisdom of God. Look at I Corinthians 1:30. "But by His doing you are in Christ Jesus, who became to us _____ from God, and righteousness and sanctification, and redemption."

Jesus was also with God in the beginning. He is worth far more than jewels and by Him kings reign. Power is his; those who seek Him find Him; wealth and righteousness are his; etc. Find some New Testament verses that answer the Old Testament riddle. You may use a concordance.

Jesus was with God in the beginning <u>John 1:1, 1 John 1:1-3</u>

Righteousness is His. _____

Power is His. _____

Those who seek Him find Him. _____

Wealth is His. _____

His mouth will utter truth. _____

He wants to endow those who love Him with wealth, to fill their treasuries. _____

Blessed are those who keep His ways. _____

Those who hate Him love death. _____

Those who find Him find life. _____

Be ready to recite Proverbs 3:1-16 tomorrow.

Questions to think about:

1. Write about a time when the character of Jesus showed you wisdom through a situation.

2. Say Proverbs 3:1-10.

> My son …
> But let your …
> Or …
> And …
> Do not let …
> Bind …
> Write …
> So you will …
> In the …
> Trust …
> And do not …
> In all …
> And He …
> Do not be …
> Fear …
> It will be …
> And …
> Honor …
> And from …
> So your …
> And your …

Week 6 Group Discussion

1. Are your words bringing life or death to others? (Prov. 15:1, 18:21, 21:23, 25:11).

2. How is being a Christian like a soldier? An athlete? A farmer? (, Is. 28:24-29, 1 Cor. 9:24-27, 2 Tim. 2:3-6, 4:7, James 5:7).

3. Which of these metaphors challenges you the most?

4. Your mind can only think on one thing at a time. When you are tempted by the things of this world, share a verse of Scripture you can meditate on to keep your mind focused on God? (Rom. 12:2, Phil. 4:8, Col. 3:2).

5. If you are born again, you are no longer a caterpillar, but a butterfly. Are you soaring in the clouds or still trying to get up off the ground? What is the means to getting launched? (1 John 3:16, Matt. 4:17).

6. Why should you who are forgiven from your sins, no longer live in sin? (John 8:11, Rom. 6:1-7, 6:22, Gal. 5:22).

7. God is like a father, only perfect. This makes you His son or daughter. How does God respond to His children's sin? (Psalm 103:8-14, Matthew 23:37, Mark 3:5, 11:15).

8. Share a time when the character of Jesus showed you wisdom through a situation.

9. Possible answers to Lesson Week 6 Day 5 New Testament verses that answer the Old Testament riddle.

10. Recite Proverbs 3:1-14 aloud.

Renewing Your Mind

Blessed is the man who listens to me,
Watching daily at my gates,
Waiting at my doorposts.
For he who finds me finds life
And obtains favor from the Lord.

PROVERBS 8:34-35

You learned last week that Jesus is the personification of wisdom. Wisdom was laid down before time and before creation, in essence, wisdom is the very character of God. Here it is—absolute truth.

Our society is twisting truth to fit each one's circumstances, personality, desires, etc. But, God's Word stands and truth was established from the beginning and exists outside of human experience. Wisdom comes in only one flavor—Truth—absolute truth at that! Truth is honesty because God is honest. Truth is justice because God is just. Truth is pure because God is pure. Truth is eternal and unchanging because God is eternal and unchanging.

Wisdom, then, is a stable foundation. Jesus is a stable foundation. Truth is a stable foundation. If you build your life, your relationships, your dreams, your desires, your expectations, upon this wisdom, you will stand firm. It's not a secret. Wisdom calls out from the heights, from beside the way, at the entrance of doors. So, why are so many blind and deaf to her call?

According to Ephesians 4:17-19 how did the Gentiles walk? _____

They were "Being darkened in their understanding, excluded from the life of God because of the ignorance that is in them, because of the hardness of their heart; and they, having become _____
have given themselves over to sensuality for the practice of every kind of impurity with greediness."

And in Romans 1:21-25, people knew God, but did not _____Him or give Him _____ _____. "And their foolish hearts were _____. Professing to be wise, they became _____."

These verses say they "Exchanged the truth of God for a lie." God's mercy and grace is available to all, but one must reach out and accept it. Huxley was a friend of Charles Darwin and one of the biggest proponents of evolutionary biology. He said, "I suppose the reason we leaped at The Origin of Species was because the idea of God interfered with our sexual mores." [31]

Huxley could not believe in Christianity even though evolution had no proof because then he would have to change his amoral (without morals) lifestyle. Man's unwillingness to submit to God's rules and laws under His redeeming grace keeps them in the dark. They are throwing away the treasure for temporary pleasure (Heb.11:25).

1 Corinthians 2:14 says, "A natural man does not accept the things of the Spirit of God, for they are _____ _____to him, he cannot understand them because they are spiritually appraised." When the Holy Spirit comes to live in your life, He brings spiritual wisdom and light. You can begin to see things differently; you are made new; your mind is renewed when you seek God through Scripture and prayer for you have the mind of Christ (1 Cor. 2:16).

I have been working with a young lady who was raped by her cousin when she was just 14 years old. She later became a Christian and mourned the fact she was not a virgin. However, in Christ there is now no condemnation (Romans 8:1) and before Him she is now a new creature, pure and righteous. She needs to understand this and begin to renew her mind with His promises and accept herself as Christ has declared her—holy and perfect. Are you still accepting Satan's accusations for sins you committed before you accepted Jesus as your Savior? _____

Shame should be laid at the cross along with sin. Adam and Eve knew shame only after they had sinned. Shame is connected to sin. You laid your sin at the cross. Leave your shame there as well, and when Satan accuses, declare the truth of your salvation.

Remember, though, renewing your mind is a choice. Renewal only happens as you spend time with God and in His Word.

Look at Proverbs 8:32-34. According to these verses you must do 7 things. What are they?

1.
2.
3.
4.

5.

6.

7.

We must hear God's Word and do it (James 1:22).

Questions to think about:

1. If someone chooses not to believe in the truth of the Bible does this make the Bible not true?

2. Are there absolute truths?

3. Name some of these absolute truths.

4. How can you "take every thought captive to the obedience of Christ"?

5. Add Proverbs 3:11 to your Appendix C.

Week 7 / Day 2

Wise Words

Blessed are they who keep my ways.
Heed instruction and be wise,
And do not neglect it.

PROVERBS 8:32-33

Find the following words in the word search on the next page.

Prudence	Discretion	Righteous	Power
Noble things	Hates evil	Knowledge	Justice
Right things	Hates pride	Understanding	Love
Truthful	Sound counsel	Jewels	Riches
Honor	Wealth	Generous	

```
G  P  R  E  G  D  E  L  W  O  N  K  H  I  N  D  V  R  T  L  S
N  E  P  O  W  S  P  D  I  S  M  E  O  N  E  W  F  T  L  L  G
I  S  N  U  N  D  J  R  I  H  O  J  N  V  E  D  L  T  E  B  N
H  O  R  E  N  T  U  L  C  S  W  L  O  R  B  S  D  W  T  H  I
S  E  D  I  R  P  S  E  T  A  H  L  R  Q  R  C  E  U  A  W  H
T  M  P  L  M  O  K  I  F  E  C  I  T  S  U  J  Y  E  H  B  T
E  R  E  O  K  O  U  N  D  E  R  S  T  A  N  D  I  N  G  G  E
A  I  C  J  L  H  J  S  G  I  R  Y  B  L  P  G  H  C  T  H  L
H  C  N  O  N  W  E  A  L  T  H  C  U  U  R  T  A  N  O  B  B
I  H  E  L  P  H  J  S  R  T  D  F  B  P  P  R  T  U  O  D  O
W  E  D  E  C  T  R  I  D  I  H  D  I  S  C  R  E  T  I  O  N
G  S  U  I  O  U  G  E  S  T  U  H  N  T  F  T  S  S  E  T  N
E  M  R  A  G  H  F  C  U  L  Y  R  L  U  R  U  E  T  C  E  V
N  T  P  I  T  O  O  R  P  M  S  E  L  S  H  R  V  A  D  U  H
N  L  L  E  P  V  T  H  O  N  O  W  L  T  G  T  I  E  R  O  A
O  P  O  M  E  S  O  U  N  D  C  O  U  N  S  E  L  W  I  P  T
U  U  S  R  T  R  M  E  D  O  W  P  B  M  C  H  N  U  O  S  E
S  R  Y  R  Q  T  P  U  N  S  G  N  I  H  T  T  H  G  I  R  S
```

Questions to think about:

1. Add characteristics and results of wisdom from chapter 8 to your charts. (I found 19).

2. Start memorizing Proverbs 3:11.

    My son, do not reject the _____ of the _____
    Or _____ His _____.

God's Inspired Words

Wisdom has built her house,
She has hewn out her seven pillars;
She has prepared her food,
She has mixed her wine;
She has also set her table.

PROVERBS 9:1-2

ead Proverbs 9:1-6. Notice how stable Wisdom seems and how her work is already done. She *has* built her house, *has* hewn out her seven pillars, *has* prepared her food, *has* mixed her wine, and *has* set her table. She is already established. This reminds me of Ephesians 4:14-15.

Write these verses: _____
_____
_____
_____
_____
_____

You, too, are to be established, grounded, unmovable according to truth, and firm in your beliefs and doctrines. You should test (discern) the spirits (1 John 4:1), take every thought captive (2 Cor. 10:5), and be willing and ready to give an account thereof in the day of judgment (Matt. 12:36).

Many believe the pillars of wisdom were doctrines adopted by the early church. These seven pillars are:

1. Salvation
2. Baptism

3. Doctrine or discipleship
4. Fellowship
5. Breaking of bread
6. Prayer
7. Giving

In Proverbs 9:2, notice that wisdom is abundantly supplied to feast and dine all who are willing to seek her out. She never runs out of resources and never has to beg or borrow from others. God's depths are fathomless. His Word is inexhaustible. You can come to the same verse or passage again and again and the Holy Spirit may reveal more depth each time. His Word speaks to your heart, mind, and emotions and will meet you where you are each time either exhorting, disciplining, training, or reminding you of His character, His promises, and His plan.

Read 2 Timothy 3:16-17. What are the four things Paul tells Timothy that Scripture is profitable for? I know you have already studied this, but this is really important.

1.
2.
3.
4.

Another word for *inspired* is God-breathed. Even though men took up the pen to write the actual words of Scripture onto paper, it was God who first put the words upon their hearts and compelled them to write giving them dictation word for word.

2 Timothy 3:17 says that Scripture is adequate, or complete, or capable and will prepare or equip us for every good work. Hebrews 13:20-21 says, "Jesus our Lord (will) equip you in every good thing to do His will, working in us that which is pleasing in His sight." His Word is the training tool equipping you to do the will of God, but the Holy Spirit is also involved as you read and study equipping you to do that which pleases God.

How important is it, then, that you study Scripture diligently and deliberately? See 2 Timothy 3:14-15. _____

Questions to think about:

1. What are you doing now that you think God is using to equip you for some future work?

2. What can you do to make Bible study more a part of every day?

3. Do you seek the Holy Spirit's wisdom before speaking the truth in love?

4. Why is this important?

5. Work on your memory verses.

> My son …
> But let your …
> For …
> And …
> Do not let …
> Bind …
> Write …
> So you will …
> In the …
> Trust …
> And do not …
> In all …
> And He …
> Do not be …
> Fear …
> It will be …
> And …
> Honor …
> And from …
> So your …
> And your …
> My son, do not _____ the _____ of the Lord Or _____ His reproof.

Week 7 / Day 4

Wisdom vs. Foolishness

The woman of folly is boisterous,
She is naïve and know nothing.

Proverbs 9:13

Proverbs chapter 9 is a sandwich with verses 1-6 contrasting verses 13-18. You will look at these today and the *meat and cheese* verses (7-12) tomorrow.

These two portions of Scripture contrast the wise woman and the foolish woman. Look through these verses and fill out the following chart.

Wise Woman   **Foolish Woman**

Character:

Placement:

Calls to whom:

Message:

Offers:

As you learned last lesson, the wise woman has a character of preparedness and completion which took diligence and single-mindedness. Compare this to the description of the woman in verse 13. It says she is a woman of folly who is boisterous. *The American Heritage Dictionary* defines "boisterous" as: 1. violent and turbulent and

2. noisy and unrestrained.[32] Compared to the wise woman, "the foolish woman is naïve and knows nothing" (Prov. 9:13).

Notice in verse 3, the wise woman unashamedly calls from the tops of the heights of the city. She is open and does not fear reprisal or an attack on her reputation, whereas the foolish woman of verse 14, "Sits at the doorway of her house on a seat by the high places of the city." She leaves herself an avenue of escape (back inside) and lingers near the high places, but doesn't venture to call out openly. Her work is best done in private.

This next point is pivotal. Look to whom each woman calls. The wise woman calls out to all who will hear. The foolish calls to those who pass by making their paths straight. Wow! Wisdom is available for everyone; foolishness tries to trap those who are righteous even though the words of their message are the same: "Whoever is naïve let him turn in here." The key is the results of their message. To those who follow wisdom and forsake folly is promised life and the way to understanding. The end result of those who follow folly is stolen water, secret bread, and death.

This lesson will wrap up your wise and foolish charts. Add Proverbs 9:1-6 and 13-18 to your charts. Take a look at what you've recorded. The choice is pretty plain, the characteristics are clear, and the results are eternal.

Questions to think about:

1. Why does the foolish woman look to trap the righteous and not the foolish?

2. Does Satan attack unbelievers or believers more? Why?

3. Almost there. Say Proverbs 3:1-11 by memory.

> My son …
> But let your …
> For …
> And …
> Do not let …
> Bind …
> Write …
> So you will …
> In the …
> Trust …
> And do not …
> In all …
> And He …

Do not be …
Fear …
It will be …
And …
Honor …
And from …
So your …
And your …
My son, do not _____ the _____ of the _____
Or _____ His _____.

Repent and Turn

> *Do not reprove a scoffer, or he will hate you,*
> *Reprove a wise man and he will love you …*
> *Give instruction to a wise man and he will be still wiser;*
> *Teach a righteous man and he will increase his learning.*
> *The fear of the Lord is the beginning of wisdom,*
> *And the knowledge of the Holy One is understanding.*
>
> *PROVERBS 9:8-10*

*H*ere's the *meat and cheese* of the sandwich which has wisdom on one side and foolishness on the other. I see these verses as a warning, an opportunity for self-evaluation, a chance to repent and turn.

Read Proverbs 9:7-9 and evaluate how you receive reproof. Do you listen and heed discipline or do you scoff at authority figures (including your husband)? _____

Do you turn and tell tales out of anger and resentment about the one who meted out the punishment or do you humble your heart and ask for forgiveness? _____
_____

I find that my response is directly relational to the respect that I have for the one in authority. If my god or my husband or a cherished friend reproves, I will receive it with humility. If someone that I don't trust or that I don't feel has the right of authority over me, I more likely to respond in anger and resentment.

Turn to Hebrews 12:4-13. Who does a father discipline? _____

According to Hebrews 12:6, what is God's motive for discipline? _____

If God does not discipline you, according to Hebrews 12:8, what are you? _____

Friend, if you do not know God's discipline, check your heart and be sure you have bowed at the cross, repented, and have received Christ as Savior and Lord. Then be discerning of the things going on around you—could it be God's training and disciplining hand?

One day in early November, I combed our apartment searching for my son. He was four-years old and the apartment was only 600 square feet. I found him by following the trail of candy wrappers to the closet. When I opened it, there sat my wide-eyed little boy with two fists full of candy and a mouth covered in chocolate and full of caramel. I wanted to laugh, but I knew this was serious. He was hiding. Just as Adam and Eve hid in the garden when they sinned, so my innocent (?) baby was hiding from his parent who loved him and wanted to bless him, not curse him. I first had to discipline out of love and for training. Eventually, he climbed back into my lap and gave me a big hug and an "I'm sorry." We were friends again and everything was good.

According to Hebrews 12:9, what should your reaction to the one who disciplines you be? _____

_____

According to Hebrews 12:10, what is God's motive for disciplining us? _____

_____

Is discipline joyful at the moment? _____

What does one trained by discipline bear in Hebrews 12:11? _____

When you encounter discipline you have a choice to make. You can either become stubborn, self-righteous, and vain which leads to rebellion, or you can humble your heart, admit your fault, and let Christ's love heal you and restore you.

What road have you been likely to take? _____

Are you willing to choose wisdom the next time discipline enters your life whether by human authority or God?

_____

Back to Proverbs 9—the litmus test is verses 8 and 9. Do you hate him who disciplines you or do you love him? _____

One response is foolish and the other wise. Understanding verse 9 can change the course of your life. Instruction and teaching is for your good; the more you can acquire, the wiser you'll be. This is not the acquisition of just facts, but rather the discerning ability that enables you to use your knowledge to avoid trouble, solve problems, reach goals, and succeed in life—from God's perspective.

Verse 10 is like Proverbs 1:7. Wisdom starts with fearing God. This is the understanding of who God is as Creator, Sustainer, and Savior. Many say this type of fear is really just knowing the awesomeness of God. I disagree; I truly believe if you saw God you would be terrified. First, because of His holiness; second, because of your sin. You should fear God's disapproval of your sin and yet be able to embrace the love He has for you. You must be able to bow before Him reverently as your King, and also be able to climb into His lap as your Father. Is this not the cross? And this is the beginning.

Proverbs 9:11 is full of God's promise. "For by me your days will be multiplied, And years of life will be added to you." This verse should remind you of your memory verses of chapter 3. Wisdom brings not only peace with God and eternal life but also the number of days and years you will be blessed with here on earth. A holy life is a healthy life!

Proverbs 9:12 is a sober reminder of reality. "If you are wise, you are wise for yourself, And if you scoff, you alone will bear it." When all is said and done, it will be you, and you alone—stripped of parents, siblings, friends, etc…, who stands before God's throne.

Questions to think about:

1. When you were little and knew you had done something you shouldn't have done, did you fear your mom or dad?

2. When you drive over the speed limit do you fear the policeman sitting on the corner?

3. When you sin, do you fear God?

4. Recite Proverbs 3:1-11.

    My son …
    But let your …
    For …
    And …
    Do not let …
    Bind …
    Write …
    So you will …
    In the …
    Trust …
    And do not …
    In all …

And He …
Do not be …
Fear …
It will be …
And …
Honor …
And from …
So your …
And your …
My son …
Or …

Week 7 Group Discussion

1. If someone chooses not to believe in the truth of the Bible does that make the Bible not true? (John 14:6).

2. Are there absolute truths? (Genesis 1:1, John 8:32).

3. Name some of these absolute truths. (God created us, God loves us, God provided a way to have a relationship with Him for eternity through the birth, life, death and resurrection of Jesus Christ, Satan is the Prince of the Power of the air, Satan will be defeated, morality does matter, etc.).

4. What are you doing now that you think God is using to equip you for some future work? (Jer. 29:11, Eph. 2:10, Phil. 1:6, 2 Tim. 2:21).

5. Why does the foolish woman (and Satan) look to trap the righteous and not the foolish? (The foolish already belong to Satan's camp. — Matt. 12:30, Eph. 2:1-7, Col. 1:13).

6. Discuss the wise and foolish charts.

7. When you drive over the speed limit do you fear the policeman sitting on the corner?

8. When you sin, do you fear God? As a Christian you do not have to fear the wrath of God (Rom. 8:1), but instead, your fear is to be a holy reverence for God. At the final judgment, all born again believers will be ushered into the kingdom of God. Will you receive a crown? (1 Cor. 9:25, 1 Thess. 2:19-20, 2 Tim. 4:8, James 1:12, 1 Peter 5:1-4).

9. Recite Proverbs 3:1-11.

Comparison of Old and New Natures

For by me your days will be multiplied,
And years of life will be added to you.
If you are wise, you are wise for yourself,
And if you scoff, you alone will bear it.

PROVERBS 9:11-12

$\mathcal{I}$n the next two days you will make another chart that will remind you a lot of your wisdom/foolishness chart. This chart will center in the New Testament and will contrast the old nature and the new nature. When you were born again into a relationship with the Father, "Old things [were] passed away and behold all things [became] new" (2 Corinthians 5:17).

Using the following verses fill in the chart on the following page. Look up each verse and determine the characteristics of the old and new natures. Determine which nature the verse is describing and turn the words into adjectives and record them under the proper heading on the next page. Try filling in the blank: I was _____or I am now _____. For example, in Galatians 5:19 there is a list of the old nature such as immorality, impurity, etc. You would record them as adjectives: "I was <u>immoral</u>"; "I was <u>impure</u>."

You have two days to finish this assignment.

Matthew	5:13-14
John	1:12-13
Romans	1:7
	5:17-18
	6:6-7

	8:1
	8:16-17
	8:37
2 Corinthians	5:17
	5:21
Galatians	5:19-21
	5:22-24
Ephesians	1:7
	2:1-3
	2:4-6
	2:10
	3:5-10
	4:17-22
	4:23-32
	6:10
Colossians	2:9-10
	3:12
Titus	3:3-7
1 Peter	1:16
	1:23
1 John	4:17

OLD NATURE   NEW NATURE

For further lists of our flesh or sin nature see my website at http://www.abidingtruthministry.com. Click on Resources. Go down to conference notes and go to *What Really Happened at the Cross* to download the *Flesh Inventory.*

Questions to think about:

1. When you were born again, you put on a new nature. How often do you need to put this nature on?

2. Does freedom in Christ mean now you can do whatever you want to? Paul says that as sinners you were a slave to sin, but now you should be a slave to righteousness.

3. One more verse, and you will have memorized Proverbs 3:1-12. Add verse 12 to your Appendix C.

Freedom from Shame

A wise son makes a father glad,
But a foolish son is a grief to his mother.

PROVERBS 10:1

*I*f you are a parent, you know the truth of this statement. We rejoice when our kids are making good decisions and mourn and grieve when they choose the way of the world. We rejoice when we see them turn from their sin, repent, and let go of shame to live productively and joyfully once again.

Take your chart from yesterday and with a marker write the word *shame* in big bold letters right across the words under Old Nature. Cover the whole length of the paper with that ugly word. Shame is the result of being an enemy of Christ. When you were born again, you no longer have to accept the feelings or truth of shame.

According to Psalm 69:19, who knows about your shame? _____

But as children of God, you have a refuge where you never need to be ashamed.

According to Psalm 71:1-3, where is this refuge? _____

Explain the following statement: "You are not a sinner because you sin, but you sin because you are a sinner."

_____

_____

_____

_____

Sure, all of us have committed sins. You have lied, or stolen, or been rebellious, or had evil thoughts about someone. Those acts and attitudes and sinful thoughts are a product of your sinful nature. You were born into sin because you were born of Adam, a sinner. I am a Rasmussen, because I was born into the Rasmussen family. I am a sinner because I was born into a sinner's family. However, when I was born again, adopted by God, I became a new creature. I am now born unto righteousness and no longer have to keep sinning. Before I sinned because I was a sinner, now when I sin, it is because I have chosen to. Jesus was not born of Adam; His father was God. Therefore, not only did He never sin, but He never was a sinner.

Would it have done any good to tell the old self to not lie, be peaceable, forgiving, etc.? Why or why not?

_____

_____

You could fake perfection or maturity for a short time, but without God, you will revert back to the old nature. Now that you have a new nature, you can choose to live according to the Word of God by the power of the Holy Spirit.

How is a victorious Christian life lived? Let me give you three steps.

1. Lay aside the old nature with its practices (Colossians 3:8).
2. Be transformed by the renewing of your mind (Romans 12:2).
3. Put on the new nature (Colossians 3:10).

In the Greek, each of these is a progressive verb. That means to keep laying aside the old nature, keep being transformed, keep always putting on the new nature. You were born again one time, but you have to keep being restored—one choice at a time.

There is power in the Word of God—power to renew your mind and to regenerate your life. Don't leave the Word on a shelf—eat of it daily and be renewed by the Holy Spirit. Then when temptations come, you have the sword (the Word of God) in your hand and ready to be used.

Take your chart and fold the old nature side to the back so all you can see is the new nature.

Across the New Nature take your marker and write *Freedom*. In Christ there is freedom to be His child and to grow up in a relationship with Christ. You are no longer bound by the law and the resulting shame.

According to Philippians 3:13-14, what are we to forget? _____

That means the past: past sins you committed, past sins committed against you, broken promises, broken dreams, unrealistic expectations, and shame.

According to these verses what are you to reach forward to? _____

That's right: the future. A future with God in control. He is waiting for you at the goal line with a prize.

Release the past, embrace the future. Prayerfully consider what you need to let go of. Write them on a piece of paper and tear it up into tiny pieces and throw it away. Satan no longer has control over you. You are a prince or princess in God's kingdom. Go forward and walk as one.

Sure, Satan will come back and remind you of the past. Remember, "That was then; this is now." The old things are passed away, and all things have become new. Remind him now that God is your King. Satan's condemnation will still come against your personhood bringing false guilt for sins that God has already declared you forgiven. The Holy Spirit will bring conviction against sin that you have not yet confessed or repented. It's important to know the difference between these voices. God will never attack you as a person, but rather discipline you so that your relationship with Him might be restored.

On the top of the New Nature list write Prince or Princess and your name. This is your position. You may not always look like a princess or act like a princess, but that doesn't change the fact that you are a daughter of the King of Kings!

Post this list on a mirror or door where you will see this truth often and remind yourself of all God has done for you. This is part of your weapon of God's word in spiritual warfare against Satan. It's no good on the shelf. You have to use it! Now would be a good time to take a minute and praise God for His goodness.

Questions to think about:

1. Does a Christian have any reason for shame from past or present actions?

2. As a princess should you become haughty and selfish or serving and graceful?

3. Make a prayer box. Use any box such as a Kleenex box and decorate it. When you have a concern you need to turn over to God, write it on a piece of paper, pray about it, and put it in the box. If you start worrying about this matter or trying to figure it out, take the piece of paper out of the box, pray, and place the situation into God's hands again by putting the paper back into the box.

4. Recite your memorized verses and work on verse 12.

    My son ...
    But let your ...
    For ...

And …
Do not let …
Bind …
Write …
So you will …
In the …
Trust …
And do not …
In all …
And He …
Do not be …
Fear …
It will be …
And …
Honor …
And from …
So your …
And your …
My son …
Or …
For whom the Lord loves He _____,
Even as a father corrects the _____ in whom he _____.

The Fear of the Lord

He who walks in his uprightness fears the Lord,
But he who is devious in his way despises Him.

PROVERBS 14:2

Do a quick review from the very beginning of this course. Fill in the blank from Proverbs 1:7. "The fear of the Lord is the beginning of _____."

Now check out Psalm 111:7-10, "The works of His hands are truth and justice; All His precepts are sure. They are upheld forever and ever; they are performed in truth and uprightness. He has sent redemption to His people; He has ordained His covenant forever; Holy and awesome is His name. The fear of the Lord is the beginning of_____ _____ ; a good understanding has all those who do His commandments; His praise endures forever."

What do you think the fear of the Lord is based on according to these verses—His terrible anger and desire to see men pay for their sins? Or His righteousness, justice, and desire to see people repent and have a relationship with Him? _____

_____

Psalm 112 will help you to answer the last question. From Psalm 112, list some of the things that will happen to the man that fears the Lord. (I found 18.)

Back to Proverbs 14:2 (see beginning of this lesson). What is the righteousness man must walk in to fear the Lord? Job found out it wasn't his own righteousness. He complained grievously before the Lord to come and hear his defense and then he was sure God would judge rightly. But when God did show up and asked a few questions of Job such as: Had Job helped to lay the foundations of the earth? Who set its measurements? Or who enclosed the seas with a door? Or have you ever in your life commanded the morning, and caused the dawn to know its place (Job 38-41)? Job realized then his righteousness was not enough to put him on equal footing with God to demand a response. He humbled himself before God.

Listen to Job's words in chapter 42.

> I know that You can do all things,
> And that no purpose of Yours can be thwarted.
> Who is this that hides counsel without knowledge?
> Therefore, I have declared that which I did not understand,
> Things too wonderful for me, which I did not know.
> Hear now, and I will speak;
> I will ask you, and You instruct me.
> I have heard of You by the hearing of the ear;
> But now my eye sees You;
> Therefore, I retract,
> And I repent in dust and ashes.

Fear of the Lord requires a humbling of the heart: a recognition of who God is; an understanding that you stand before God not in your own righteousness, but in the righteousness given to you to wear by Jesus as He died on the cross and took upon Himself your sin. (Philippians 3:9, "And may be found in Him, not having a righteousness of my own derived from the Law, but that which is through faith in Christ, the righteousness which comes from God on the basis of faith").

It is the righteous in Christ that God refers to in Proverbs 15:29: "The Lord is far from the wicked, but He hears the _____ of the righteous." For, "Who can say, 'I have cleansed my heart, I am pure from my sins'" (Prov. 20:9), except those who have been cleansed by the blood of Jesus?

Many try to relate to God through church rituals and meeting expectations put on them by their parents or the church. God is not impressed with ritual or sacrifice. Proverbs 15:8 states, "The _____ _____ of the wicked is an _____ to the Lord, but the prayer of the upright is His delight." That's right, if you are born again through your faith in Jesus then God delights in you and wants to spend time with you. He is looking forward to spending all eternity with you!

Listen to God's promise to believers in John 14:1-3: "Do not let your heart be troubled; believe in God, believe also in Me. In My Father's house are many dwelling places; if it were not so, I would have told you; for I go to prepare a place for you. If I go and prepare a place for you, I will come again and receive you to Myself, that where I am, there you may be also."

In these verses what is the prerequisite for Jesus preparing you a place and coming back for you? _____
_____

Do you have to tithe faithfully first, offer a sacrifice, or do good deeds? No. All you have to do to spend eternity with God is believe in God the Father and in Jesus. This is not believing in just the facts, even the demons believe, and yet they shudder (James 2:19). This must be the belief which motivates you to the act of praying that God will come into your life and take control.

If you fear God enough to believe His Word, you are going to heaven. Works and good deeds come after that in your gratitude and your changed heart and mind. God promises to be doing the changing in you. You have only to believe. God is so good!

You are now ready to embark on laying aside of the old nature and putting on the new nature with a practical study through Proverbs concerning various topics that concern you as God's child and will affect the rest of your life. Remember the writer of Proverbs is good King Solomon. Even though he wasn't perfect, he learned from his mistakes and sought God's wisdom. You can also.

Now look at 1 Corinthians 2:16. It says that as a believer, you have the mind of Christ.

If wisdom is the ability to judge correctly and use our knowledge to avoid trouble, solve problems, reach goals, and succeed in life based upon God's principles, then having the mind of Christ is the key. Romans 12:2 says, "Do not be conformed to this world, but be transformed by the renewing of your mind." A renewed mind is the mind of Christ. You get the mind of Christ by reading His word, talking to Jesus, and asking Him for wisdom.

Colossians 3:2 reiterates this principle. Write this verse here _____
_____

Questions to think about:

1. What is the difference between knowing about Abraham Lincoln and knowing Abraham Lincoln?

2. What is the difference between knowing about God and knowing God?

3. Pray for someone you know who knows about God, but needs to know Him personally.

4. Brush up on Proverbs 3:1-11 and keep working on 12.

> My son ...
> But let your ...
> For ...

And …
Do not let …
Bind …
Write …
So you will …
In the …
Trust …
And do not …
In all …
And He …
Do not be …
Fear…
It will be …
And …
Honor …
And from …
So your …
And your …
My son …
Or …
For whom the Lord _____ He _____,
Even as a _____ corrects the _____ in whom he _____.

Now What?

*Let the word of Christ richly dwell within you,
with all wisdom teaching and admonishing one
another .... Whatever you do in word or deed, do
all in the name of the Lord Jesus, giving thanks
through Him to God the Father.*

COLOSSIANS 3:16-17

You learned in your last lesson you can't work your way to heaven; salvation comes only through believing in Jesus. So, now what?

At our house, when the kids were little, we had one overriding rule that took precedence over all others: "Did or will an action or a word make the other person feel special?" If an action did not make the other person feel special, then it was wrong. Colossians 3:17 gives you an overriding rule for living a victorious Christian life: "Whatever you do in word or deed, do all in the name of the Lord Jesus." This is so important it is stated a few verses later. Write out Colossians 3:23. _____

_____

_____

That's right, you are to do whatever you do heartily, which means with a whole heart or effort, as for the Lord rather than men. For me, this included cleaning toilets which was no easy task with five boys and a husband! I learned to praise God for healthy boys. While ironing, I learned to pray for the person whose shirt I was pressing, asking God to press out the sin and press His righteousness into his life.

Notice in verse 17 your actions should come from a heart of thanksgiving. What should you be thankful for? Everything! First, your salvation. Second every breath you breathe. Then, every action you can perform, every blessing you receive, and, yes, every trial which comes your way. Read James 1:2-4. Yes, you are to be thankful for the trials because they are working in you to make you perfect and complete.

It all narrows down to choices. How am I going to act in this situation? How am I going to respond to this circumstance? What is my attitude going to be like in this trial? How am I going to treat my body? How am I going to speak? How am I going to spend my money? My time? How am I going to let God work in my life to control my emotions? Am I going to read my Bible? Am I going to go to that Bible study or church? Who should I marry? What should I do for a career?

You cannot always change your circumstances, but you can change your responses. It sure would be easier if God just wrote it all out for us! I used to say, "God, just give me some writing on the wall like You did for Belshazzar" (Daniel chapter 5). But then I realized that very night, God took Belshazzar's life and kingdom away! God does not spell everything out for you, because He wants you to have a relationship with Him. Lists do not require relationship. He wants you to talk to Him, share your heart with Him, listen to Him, and obey Him. Finishing a list of to-do's might be easier, but getting to know your Father and Savior is even better.

Look back at your verses in Colossians. In Colossians 3:16 what must richly dwell within you?

_____

_____

How must the Word of God dwell within you? _____

What does that look like? It means you are reading, studying, asking questions, memorizing, meditating upon and praying through the Word of God. Wisdom takes time, it takes commitment, but only through the Word shall you be transformed (Romans 12:2) and have the mind of Christ (1 Corinthians 2:16). With the mind of Christ, according to Colossians 3:16, you will have wisdom and will be able to admonish and encourage others.

Practical Proverbs for Women: Living Gracefully will help you to know how you are to walk and work doing all things for and through Jesus.

Questions to think about:

1. What is one chore or task you have a hard time doing heartily as unto the Lord?

2. What praise song might you sing while doing this task that would make it more enjoyable?

3. Is God more interested in you getting your tasks done or your heart attitude as you do it?

4. Last day to perfect those memory verses.

My son …
But let your …
For …
And …
Do not let …
Bind …
Write …
So you will …
In the …
Trust …
And do not…
In all …
And He …
Do not be …
Fear …
It will be …
And …
Honor …
And from …
So your …
And your …
My son …
Or …
For whom …
Even as …

Week 8 Group Discussion

1. When you were born again, you were given a new nature. How often do you need to put this nature on? (It is yours when you choose to accept Jesus as Lord and Savior – Rom. 10:9-10. Now you must practice using it–Col. 3:12-14).

2. Does freedom in Christ mean now you can do whatever you want to? (Rom. 6:1-2, 1 Corinthians 6:12, 10:23).

3. Does a Christian have any reason for shame from past actions? (Shame is directly related to sin. The sin was forgiven, so you no longer have to carry around your shame. It, too, must be laid at the foot of the cross. – Gen. 3:7, 10, Ps. 69:19, 2 Cor. 4:2, Phil.1:20, 1 John 2:28).

4. Does a Christian have any reason for shame from present actions? (Conviction is from the Holy spirit, condemnation is from Satan, shame is Satan's scam–Eph. 4:1, 5:1-7, 1 John 1:9).

5. How many times this week have you put a paper into your prayer box? (Week 8 Day 3).

6. What is the difference between knowing about God and knowing God? (Only knowing God requires a relationship–Ps. 46:10, James 2:19).

7. Pray for someone you know who knows about God, but needs to know Him personally.

8. Recite Proverbs 3:1-12 aloud.

Foolishness: Characteristics and Results

	Characteristics	**Results**
1:7	despises wisdom and instruction	takes away life of its possessor

Characteristics   **Results**

Characteristics   **Results**

Characteristics   **Results**

Wisdom: Characteristics and Results

<u>Characteristics</u>   **<u>Results</u>**

Characteristics   **Results**

149

Characteristics   **Results**

Characteristics   **Results**

Proverbs 3:1-12 (NASB)

1 My son, do not forget my teaching,
But let your heart keep my commandments;

2 For length of days and years of life
And peace they will add to you.

3 Do not let kindness and truth leave you,
Bind them around your neck,
Write them on the tablet of your heart.

4 So you will find favor and good repute
In the sight of God and man.

5 Trust in the Lord with all your heart
And do not lean on your own understanding.

6 In all your ways acknowledge Him,
And He will make your paths straight.

7 Do not be wise in your own eyes;
Fear the Lord and turn away from evil.

8 It will be healing to your body
And refreshment to your bones.

9 Honor the Lord from your wealth
And from the first of all your produce;

10 So your barns will be filled with plenty
And your vats will overflow with new wine.

11 My son, do not reject the discipline of the Lord
Or loathe His reproof,

12 For whom the Lord loves He reproves,
Even as a father corrects the son in whom he delights.

Leader's Guide

Week 1
Week 1/Day 1: Wisdom, Knowledge, Instruction

When you hear the word *God* what is the image you see or words you think? __**Answers will vary**__

Write what reminds you of wisdom. _____**Answers will vary**_____

What in your life is true? _____**Answers will vary**_____

What in your life is right? _____**Answers will vary**_____

What in your life is lasting? _____**Answers will vary**_____

Mark the following which would be defined as wisdom.

_____1. Learning the names of the constellations
__**X**__2. Knowing lying is wrong and choosing to be truthful
_____3. Knowing what is for dinner
__**X**__4. Saying no to watching inappropriate movies or television shows
__**X**__5. Finding joy in spending time with God

Wisdom: **The ability to judge correctly and use our knowledge to avoid trouble, solve problems, reach goals, and succeed in life based upon God's principles.**

Knowledge: **Having the facts**

Instruction: **Putting information in order; preparing, teaching, arranging, and building up information so it can be utilized**

Questions to think about:

1. What is the difference between wisdom and knowledge? **Knowledge is having the facts whereas wisdom is using the facts to make godly, biblical decisions.**

2. Are you making wise decisions at work? In friendships? In family relationships? **Answers will vary**

3. How is your working definition of wisdom different than the world's view of wisdom? (See 1 Corinthians 1:18 -2:16.) **The world sees wisdom as avoiding trouble, solving problems, reaching goals, and succeeding in life based upon their own rules and using whatever means they want to justify the end. Our definition is based upon God's rules and His definition of success.**

4. What knowledge is biblical wisdom based on? **The Bible, but ultimately the very nature of God which includes the absolute truths set down in Scripture.**

5. Are you spending time studying the Bible to gain knowledge of God? **Answers will vary.**

Week 1/Day 2 Discernment, Prudence, Discretion

In what areas do you practice discernment? __**Answers might include in relationships, in   money management, in spiritual issues, parenting, etc.**__

What are you naïve about? Does your naivety cause problems? __**Answers will vary**__

Discernment: **being able to distinguish between good and evil, leading you to act with wisdom**

Prudence: **being wise in handling practical matters, careful about one's conduct**

Naïve: **having no knowledge, or having received knowledge refusing to apply it to one's own life with wisdom**

Discretion: **thinking about and applying wisdom before thoughts come out in words or actions**

Questions to think about:

1. How does discernment relate to wisdom? **One must have biblical knowledge to be discerning in God's wisdom in order to discern between good and bad.**

2. Are you maturing in discernment? **Answers will vary**

3. What type of discernment are you good at applying? **Answers will vary**

4. Are you prudent in areas of modesty? Speech? Dress? **Answers will vary**

5. We tell our kids, "Just because a is in your mind, doesn't mean it needs to come out of your mouth." Is this a problem for you? **Answers will vary**

6. In what situation might you need prudence? **Choosing a swimsuit, deciding how to spend your money, or deciding how to spend your time, etc.**

7. In what situation might you need discernment? **In choosing friends, in parenting, in choosing books and movies, etc.**

8. In what situation might you need discretion? **In a group of differing beliefs, on social media, in an argument, etc.**

9. Work on memorizing the working definition of wisdom.

   "Wisdom is the ability to __**judge**__ correctly and use your __**knowledge**__ to avoid trouble, solve problems, reach goals, and succeed in life based upon __**God's**__ principles."

Week 1/Day 3: Pop Quiz

1. Proverbs was written by
   b. King Solomon

2. Wisdom is the ability to judge correctly and use your knowledge to avoid trouble, solve problems, reach goals, and succeed in life based upon __**God's**__ principles.

3. According to the above definition what must be acquired before wisdom can be obtained?
   d. Knowledge

4. How do you get knowledge about God's wisdom?
   e. All of the above

5. Instruction is gained by taking the **Word** of **God** and learning how it can be applied; knowing how others have used God's words and principles, and how God honored their obedience and faithfulness in their lives.

6. True or False? There is only one type of discernment. **False**

7. True or False? Discernment is a gift you either have or don't have; it can't be gained. **False**

8. How can you get discernment?
    b. You have to exercise it.

9. True or False? You should make fun of someone who is a "prude." **False**

10. True or False? You should have prudence and, thus, you should be a prude **True**

11. True or False? Sometimes it's okay to be naïve. **True**

12. It's okay to be naïve about:
    b. Automobile engines

13. True or False? Discretion says if I know the answer I should always belt it right out. **False**

How did you do? Are you a little wiser or do you just know more? **Answers will vary**

Questions to think about:

1. Explain how the fear of the Lord is the beginning of wisdom. Relate this verse to your own life. **When we have a healthy understanding of Who God is as our Creator, King, Lord, Sustainer, etc., we should have a healthy fear of His power and rights. As a believer this fear should also include a reverence and awe of Who He is and His mercy and grace towards us.**

2. Are you daily seeking to gain wisdom? How? **Reading the Bible, listening to sermons, praying, reading about other Christians, discussing with more mature Christians, etc.**

3. Who in your life is an example of a wise person? **Answers will vary**

4. Work on memorizing the working definition of wisdom.

"Wisdom is the ability to __**judge**__ correctly and use your __**knowledge**__ to avoid __**trouble**__ , solve problems, reach__**goals**__ , and succeed in life based upon __**God's principles**__ ."

5. Begin memorizing Proverbs 1:7.

6. Read Proverbs 1:1-7 and fill in the blanks.

The proverbs of Solomon, the son of David, king of Israel:
To know __**wisdom**__ and __**instruction**__ ,
To __**discern**__ the sayings of __**understanding**__ ,
To receive __**instruction**__ in wise behavior,
Righteousness, justice and equity;
To give __**prudence**__ to the __**naive**__ ,
To the youth __**knowledge**__ and __**discretion**__ ,
A wise man will hear and increase in learning,
And a man of __**understanding**__ will acquire wise counsel,
To understand a proverb and a figure,
The words of the wise and their riddles.
The fear of the Lord is the beginning of __**knowledge**__ ;
Fools despise __**wisdom**__ and __**instruction**__ .

Week 1/Day 4: David's Choices

In 1 Samuel 8:7-9, whom had Israel rejected: God or Samuel? __**God**__

In 1 Samuel 8:7-9, what was Israel's great sin? __**forsaking God and serving other gods**__

What characteristic would the new king have?__**Would be a man after God's own heart**__
David was just a shepherd boy when Samuel anointed him king. Read 1Samuel 16:7, 12-13. Man looks at the outer appearance of men, but what does God look at? __**the heart**__

When David was anointed king, what came upon him mightily? __**the Spirit of the Lord**__

List the six attributes used to describe David.

1. **skillful musician**   4. **prudent in speech**
2. **mighty man of valor**   5. **handsome**
3. **a warrior**   6. **Lord was with him**

To what does God attribute David's success? __God place him as a ruler over Israel, God was with David, and God cut off David's enemies.__

Who is prophesied of in 2 Samuel 7: 12, 13, 16? __Solomon / Jesus__

David responded with praise and humility. Read 2 Samuel 7:18-29. Whom did David ask God to magnify? __God__

David, however, soon fell to temptation and committed adultery and murder. God again spoke to David through Nathan. Read 2 Samuel 12:1-12. Who was the rich man in this parable? __David__

David repented. Read 2 Samuel 12:13 and Psalm 51. You can see the consequences of his sin in 2 Samuel 12:14, 18a and Psalm 38. What were some of the consequences of David's sin? __death of the child, understanding of sin and feeling of being unclean and separated from God, guilt, illness, sorrow, unrest, sorrow, anxiety__

David praised God (2 Samuel 22-23:7), and Solomon reigned after David's death and brought Israel to its Golden Age. In these verses, David claims God as whose rock, fortress, deliverer, God, refuge, shield, horn of salvation, stronghold, and savior? __David's "My"__

Listen now to David's last words to Solomon. Read 1 Kings 2:2-4. If Solomon keeps God's laws, statutes, commandments, and testimonies, what will be Solomon's reward? __success in all that he does and wherever he turns__

What will be his sons' rewards? __shall not lack a man on the throne__

Questions to think about:

1. Jesus died for your sins. Does this include adultery and murder? Is He able to forgive all sins? **(*Sin* literally means missing the mark. Whether you miss the mark by an inch or a mile, you still missed it. Our *mark* is God's perfection and holiness and purity. As a creature born with a sin nature, each of us have missed the mark. The punishment is the same. The salvation price is the same – Jesus' blood. It covers all sin for those who repent.)**

2. What was David's reaction to his sin? How do you react when you are confronted with your sin? **(He was grieved, heartbroken, remorseful, and he repented.)**

3. What consequences are you bearing because of sin? **Answers will vary**

4. Are you quick to repent when you have sinned? **Answers will vary**

5. Work on your memorized definition of wisdom.

    "Wisdom is the __**ability**__ to __**judge**__ correctly and use your __**knowledge**__ to avoid __**trouble**__, solve __**problems**__, reach __**goals**__, and succeed __**in**__ __**life**__ based upon __**God's**__ __**principles**__."

6. Work on memorizing Proverbs 1:7.

    "The fear of the Lord is the __**beginning**__ of __**knowledge**__; __**fools**__ despise __**wisdom**__ and __**instruction**__."

Week 1/Day 5: Solomon's Whole-Heartedness

Read 1 Kings 3:1-15, 4:29-34. In 1 Kings 3:3 what was Solomon's motivation for obeying God? __**his love for God, an understanding heart**__

In 1 Kings 3:9, what did Solomon ask of God? __**to help him to judge God's people, to discern between good and evil**__

In verses 10-14, what was God's response? __**It pleased God. God gave him a wise and discerning heart (vs. 12) and also riches and honor (vs. 13)**__

What was the condition God put upon His promise? __**Solomon was to walk in God's way, keep God's statutes and commandments**__

In 1 Kings 8:22-24, Solomon first offers __**praise**__ (vs. 23) to God. Then he asks God to keep His __**covenant**__ (vs.25) and to have __**lovingkindness**__ (vs.28, 30, 32) upon the people and to __**forgive**__ (vs. 36) their sins.

In 1 Kings 8:40, how were the people to respond to God's just judgments and forgiveness? __**with the fear of the Lord**__

Solomon then blessed the people. Read 1 Kings 8:55-61. In 1 Kings 8:60, why was it so important the people walk in God's ways? __**Other nations will know that the Lord is God; there is no other.**__

According to verse 61, how much of your heart does God want? __**All of it.**__

God responds to Solomon with a promise and a warning (1 Kings 9:1-9). In 1 Kings 9:4-5, what are the conditions of God's promise? __Solomon must walk in God's way in integrity of heart and uprightness, doing all that God commanded, and he must keep God's statues and God's ordinances.__

In 1 Kings 9:6-7, what would lead God to cut Israel off from the land and to destroy the nation? __If Solomon or his sons turn away from following God, and do not keep God's commandments and statutes, if they go and serve other gods and worship them.__

You will find even Solomon, with God's wisdom, falters and falls. Read 1 Kings 11:1-6.
What was Solomon's sin? __Taking more than one wife and following their gods; not being wholly devoted to the Lord.__

He repents, but not before he, too, is told the consequences of his sins. Read 1 Kings 11:9-13. What are the consequences of his sin? __God would tear the kingdom from him and give it to his servant.__

An autobiography of Solomon's life, the book of Ecclesiastes, ends with great words of wisdom. In Ecclesiastes 12:9-14, what did Solomon conclude at the end of his life? __Fear God and keep His commandments because this applies to every person.__

Questions to think about:

1. Why do you obey God? **(Answers will vary but may include: It's the right thing to do, It is my duty, I want to go to heaven, in praise for what Jesus did for me, because He is God, etc.)**

2. When you sin do you quickly ask God to forgive you? **Answers will vary**

3. Is there any sin too big for God to forgive? **No – David committed murder and adultery and was forgiven/**

4. Are you holding on to any areas of your heart (unforgiveness, bitterness, fear, control)? **Answers will vary**

5. In what areas of life are you living in your own power? **Ex: marriage, parenting, other relationship, money, future, body image, health, time management, dreams, etc.**

6. In what areas of life are you living in God's power? **Same as above**

7. Know your definition of wisdom.

"Wisdom is the __ability__ to __judge__ correctly and use your __knowledge__ to __avoid__ __trouble__, __solve__ __problems__, __reach__ __goals__, and succeed __in__ __life__ based upon __God's__ __principles__."

8. Keep working on memorizing Proverbs 1:7.

The fear of the __Lord__ is the __beginning__ of __wisdom__; __fools__ despise __wisdom__ and __instruction__.

Week 1 Group Discussion

The following questions were posed after the lessons this past week. Take time to discuss the answers and ask for responses. Additional verses are listed which will give you, the teacher, more insight. These lists are not exhaustive. Feel free to pray and ask God for other verses that answer these questions for you. You can study these ahead of time and then either ask the students to look them up during class or just refer to them as you speak.

1. What is the difference between wisdom and knowledge? (Wisdom: Matt. 13:54, Luke 21:15, 1 Cor. 1:30, 1 Cor. 12:8. Knowledge: Phil. 1:9, Col. 2:3, James 1:5, Peter 1:2-3, 5-8, 3:18) **Knowledge is limited to my human experience. Wisdom comes from God and His eternal ever-reaching Creator knowledge. When I see things from God's perspective rather than by my limited knowledge, then I am using wisdom.**

2. How does discernment relate to wisdom? (Phil. 1:9-11, Heb. 5:14) **When I am seeing and understanding my world through God's perspective, then He will open my eyes to greater understanding into human nature and the spirit world so that I can discern right and wrong, evil and good.**

3. How is your working definition of wisdom different than the world's view of wisdom? (1 Cor. 1:18-31, 2:6-10, 1 John 2:16-17) **The world views wisdom from a logical stand point or based on what seems to be right in their own eyes. Biblical wisdom is based on the facts of God and His word.**

4. What knowledge is biblical wisdom based on? (1 Cor. 1:18-31, 2:6-10) **God's word and God's character and truth.**

5. Explain how the fear of the Lord is the beginning of wisdom. Relate this verse to your own life. (Fear: reverence, awe, giving God His proper place as Creator, King, Lord, Master: Ps. 111:10, Eccl. 5:6-7, James 3:7-8) **Only when we realize the omnipotent power of the Creator do we realize our own inability to save ourselves. This fear of who God is and what He can and has the right**

to do is fearful. We may also begin the Christian walk with a fear of hell. Either way, it leads us to seek truth and find wisdom.

6. Why do you obey God? (John 14:15, John 15:10, Rev. 14:12) **Because we love God and want to abide in His love. He also promises the perseverance of the saints who keep His commandments.**

7. Is there any sin too big for God to forgive? (David committed murder and adultery, the thief on the cross, Rom. 10:9-11, 1 John 1:9) **No. Sin is missing the mark of perfection. It doesn't matter by how much we miss that mark, we have all sinned. God requires a repentant heart by everyone for every deed.**

8. What should your reaction to sin be? (Ps. 51, 1 John 1:9, 2 Cor. 7:9-11) **Sin should disgust us, and we should be repulsed by it.**

9. How do you let God lead you rather than living in your own power? (Surrender, yield, Lordship, Prov. 3:5-6, Rom. 12:2, Eph. 4;1, 5:1, 4:14-15, 22-24) **God will lead first through expecting us to live up to the moral code of His word and convicting us of our sin when we fail. Then He leads through His word, His quiet voice, circumstances, peace and sometimes through others.**

10. Give examples from your life of using wisdom according to the definition.

11. Recite together the working definition of wisdom and Proverbs 1:7.

Week 2
Week 2/Day 1: The Beginning of Wisdom

Romans 3:10 claims, "There is none righteous, no not __**one**__."

Romans 3:23 continues "__**All**__ have sinned and fall short of the glory of God." Your God is holy (set apart and perfect). You cannot stand in His presence and have sin in your life.

Therefore, from the beginning of time, a blood sacrifice was required for the *covering up* of sins.

Romans 6:23 states, "The wages of sin is __**death**__." We have all sinned, (literally meaning we have "missed the mark") and therefore, we all deserve death (eternal separation from God). The rest of that verse, however, brings hope and joy.

The second part of Romans 6:23 says, "But the __**free**____**gift**__ of God is eternal life in Christ Jesus our Lord."

What must I do to be saved? Romans 10:9-10 says, "If you confess with your mouth Jesus as Lord and believe in your heart that God raised Him from the dead, you __**will**____**be**____**saved**__."

Peter says in 1 Peter 1:3, "Blessed be the God and Father of our Lord Jesus Christ, who according to His great mercy has caused us to be __**born**____**again**__ to a living hope through the resurrection of Jesus Christ from the dead, to obtain an inheritance which is imperishable and undefiled and will not fade away, reserved in heaven for you, who are protected by the power of God through faith for a salvation ready to be revealed in the last time."

Read Romans 6:1-18. Salvation is a new birth, but in Romans 6:1 salvation is also a death. What are you to die to? __**sin**__

Baptism is a symbol of that death and new birth. According to Romans 6:4 what is the result of this death and birth? "So we too might walk in __**newness**____**of**____**life**__." Verse 7 is key. "For he who has died is __**dead**____**to**____**sin**__."

Questions to think about:

1. Put these verses in order as you would tell someone how to get to God.

Romans 6:23b	**answer top to bottom of chart:**	**Romans 10:9-10**
Romans 10:9-10		**Romans 6:23b**
Romans 3:23		**Romans 6:23a**
Romans 6:23a		**Romans 3:23**
Romans 3:10		**Romans 3:10**

2. Have you accepted Jesus Christ as your Lord and Savior? Tell about that experience.

3. How has knowing Jesus changed your heart? **Answers may vary but may include: no longer angry, feel loved, no guilt feelings, hope for eternity, hope for this life, seeking God's purpose and plan, etc.**

4. Who can you pray for and share the gospel of Jesus with using the Roman Road?

5. Keep memorizing Proverbs 1:7.

> "The __**fear**__ of the __**Lord**__ is the __**beginning**__ of __**knowledge**__ ; __**fools**__ despise __**wisdom**__ and __**instruction**__ ."

Week 2/Day 2: God's Rules

Can you or any man keep all of the rules of the Old Testament or even just the 10 commandments? Yes or No? __**No**__

Is trying your best and keeping most of the rules good enough to earn your way to heaven and give you a clear conscience? Yes or No? __**No**__

Romans 8:1 is a key verse. "Therefore there is now no __**condemnation**__ for those who are in Christ Jesus."

1 John 1:9 says, "If we __**confess our sins**__, He is faithful and just to forgive us of our sins and cleanse us from all unrighteousness."

List the top five rules you live by:

1. **Answers will vary but may include: always be on time, don't be easily offended, always put on make-up before going out, etc.**
2.
3.
4.
5.

Look up and define these words:

COMMANDMENTS: **a command: an edict**
LAWS: **rules established by authority, society, or custom**

PRECEPTS: **a general rule intended to regulate behavior or thought**
STATUTES: **a law enacted by legislative body; a decree or edict; an established rule**
TESTIMONIES: **a declaration or affirmation of fact or truth**

Read Psalm 19:7-14 and fill in the following chart.

	God's Word	Is what?	Accomplishing what?
1.	The law of the Lord	Perfect	Restoring the soul
2.	**The testimony of the Lord**	**Sure**	**Making wise the simple**
3.	**The precepts of the Lord**	**Right**	**Rejoicing the heart**
4.	**The commandment of the Lord**	**Pure**	**Enlightening the eyes**
5.	**The fear of the Lord**	**Clean**	**Enduring forever**
6.	**The judgment of the Lord**	**True**	**Righteous**

Questions to think about:

1. What rules did your parents give you as a child you did not understand at the time but later came to see as protection or provision. **Answers will vary but may include not staying out late, not playing with someone, only having friends over when mom and dad were home, etc.**

2. God gave the rules in the Old Testament for five reasons. Read each of these reasons below and give an example of an OT rule that fits the first three.
   a. God's provision **Answers will vary but may include: only collecting enough manna for the day, what to take on the exile journey, etc.**
   b. God's protection **Answers will vary but may include: food laws, laws for criminals, etc.**
   c. That we might know God's character. **Answers will vary but may include: Thou shall have no other God besides Me, Thou shall keep the Sabbath holy, etc.**
   d. That we would realize that we could not keep the laws
   e. That we would realize that we needed a Savior

3. Look at the list of what God's Word accomplishes, and explain how one of these is being accomplished in your life.

   His law when followed brings no guilt. I need to stay confessed up and be repentant when I sin against God's law.

   His testimony is sure and can be trusted. It makes the simple wise. I gain wisdom by learning of His testimony and putting my faith in Him.

The precepts of the Lord are right and as I allow them to regulate my behavior the consequences fill my heart with joy.

The commandment of the Lord is pure. What He expects of me enlightens my eyes to His provision and protection.

The fear of the Lord is clean. Worship and reverence and fear of God's judgment and power will make me walk in the the pure and clean way which will bring eternal life.

The judgment of the Lord is true because He is truth. His judgment is based upon Jesus' sacrifice of blood and through it I am righteous.

4. Keep memorizing Proverbs 1:7.

"The **fear** of the **Lord** is the **beginning** of **knowledge** ; **fools** **despise** **wisdom** and **instruction** ."

Week 2/Day 3: Written to a Son

Look first at Proverbs 1:8-10. To whom was Solomon writing? **his son**

Proverbs:

1:8	son	6:3	son
1:10	son	6:20	son
1:15	son	7:1	son
2:1	son	7:24	son
3:1	son	8:32	son
4:1	son	23:15	son
4:10	son	23:19	son
4:20	son	23:26	son
5:1	son	24:13	son
5:20	son	24:21	son
6:1	son	27:11	son

Look at Proverbs 2:1-5. The ultimate end of a man's search is to discern the fear of the Lord and to discover the knowledge of God. Continuing on in verses 2:6-22, Solomon reveals why this is so important. God will be a **shield** (vs. 7) to those who walk with integrity, He will **preserve** (vs. 8) the ways of His godly ones, He will **deliver** (vs. 12) you from the way of evil, and then you will live in the land and remain in it—heaven forever.

Read each verse and write why Solomon wrote it to his son.

1:8-9 -	graceful wreath to your head and an ornament about your neck
3:1 -	length of days & years of life and peace
3:4 -	to find favor and good repute in the sight of God and man
3:6 -	God will make your paths straight
3:8 -	it will be healing to your body and refreshment to your bones
3:21 -	life to your soul and adornment to your neck
3:23 -	to walk in way securely and foot will not stumble
3:24 -	to not be afraid to sleep peacefully (or sweet)
4:6 -	wisdom will guard you and watch over you
4:8 -	wisdom will exalt you, she will honor you
4:10 -	years of life will be many
4:20-22 -	they are life and health
6:22 -	words will guide you, watch over you, talk to you
6:24 -	will keep you from the evil woman and the tongue of the adulteress (sin)
7:5 -	will keep you from an adulteress (sin)
8:32 -	to be wise
22:18 -	it will be pleasant and they will be ready on your lips
22:21 -	will make you know the certainty of the words of truth to correctly answer him who sends you
23:15 -	to make your father glad
23:24-25 -	make father and mother rejoice and be glad
24:14 -	for a future and hope

Questions to think about:

1. If you were a father or mother writing to your son or daughter, what advice would you give him/her? **Answers will vary.**

2. What good advice did you receive from your parents? Be specific. **Answers will vary.**

3. Keep memorizing Proverbs 1:5. "The _____**fear**_____ of the _____**Lord**_____ is the _____**beginning**_____ of __**knowledge**__; _____**fools**_____ despise **wisdom** and **instruction**_____."

4. You should have Proverbs 1:7 pretty much memorized by now. You are going to start on a longer portion of Scripture Proverbs 3:1-12. Don't worry. You will have until the end of this study to finish it, and you will be receiving help along the way. You will find these verses in Appendix C. For today, just read through these verses.

Week 2/Day 4: Definition of a Biblical Fool

According to these verses what does a fool say in his heart? _____**There is no God.**_____

"But the things that proceed out of the mouth comes from the __**heart**__ and those defile the man."

Questions to think about:

1. Explain this comment: sins committed do not make you a sinner, but rather your sin nature makes you sin? **Sin is the natural symptom of who we are before being redeemed through the blood of Jesus. Our sin nature causes us to sin. You don't have to teach a two-year old to sin; he does it by nature.**

2. If that statement is true, then why must you be born again and not just forgiven? **Forgiveness is applied to each individual sin. Before we are born again in Christ, we might gain forgiveness for a particular act, but we don't have the power to stop sinning; it is our nature. When we are born again, our new nature is one of truth and freedom from sin. Now we have a choice and can be held accountable for each choice as we have the power not to sin. We are forgiven for all of our sins. Confession and repentance brings us back into fellowship with God.**

3. Think of someone you know or someone famous who has the characteristics of a fool.

4. Begin memorizing Proverbs 3:1. If you learn with pictures, turn to Appendix C and draw pictures for *teaching* and *commandments*. (I drew a book and a set of stone commandments.) If colors help you more, you can highlight the words *teaching* and *commandments*. I also learn by doing, so making up some motions to go with the words can help as well.

Week 2/Day 5: Characteristics of a Fool

Hebrews 11:25 says, "Choosing rather to endure ill-treatment with the people of God than to enjoy the ____ **passing**_____**pleasures**_____of sin."

His motive was pure as seen in verse 26: "Considering the reproach of Christ _**greater**__ riches than the treasures of Egypt; for he was looking to the reward."

But don't forget sin leads to __**death**___ (Rom. 6:23 and James 1:14-15).

Read Proverbs 2:16-19, 5:3-6, 6:26-35, and 7:6-27 and fill in the blanks.

> "For her house sinks down to __**death**____
> And her tracks lead to the __**dead**___."

"Her feet go down to __**death**__ ,
Her steps take hold of __**Sheol**__ ." (the grave).

"The one who commits adultery with a woman is lacking sense;
He who would __**destroy**__ himself does it."

"So he does not know that it will cost him his __**life**__ ."

These verses all state that adultery (friendship with the world) will lead to __**death**__ .

Moses teaches the Israelites in Deuteronomy 6:5 to, "Love the Lord your God with __**all**__ your heart and with __**all**__ your soul and with __**all**__ your might."

Questions to think about:

1. Using Jan Silvious' definition of a fool, write about a time you acted the part of a fool. How could following Deuteronomy 6:5 have prevented those foolish notions? **Answers will vary.**

2. The Bible states that God is a jealous God. How does this relate to the nation of Israel being an adulteress? How should this impact your life? **God is jealous of His bride and wants her to be intimate– spiritually worshipping and communing– with only Him. Israel chose to worship other gods made of wood and metal. They were not faithful to the One who loved them and called them His own. I need to make sure that my love is not divided, but that I love God with all my heart, mind, and soul. The love I have for others comes from God. I worship Him only and except the others that I love as His gift.**

3. Praise God in prayer that even though you sometimes act the fool, you are forgiven.

4. Work on memorizing Proverbs 3:1-2. Highlight key words or add pictures for "length" (a ruler), "day" (a sun), "years" (a calendar), and "peace" (a peace sign).

    My son, do not forget my __**teaching**__ ,
    But let your heart keep my __**commandments**__ ;
    For length of __**days**__ and __**years**__ of life
    And __**peace**__ they will add to you.

Week 2 Group Discussion

The following questions were posed after the lessons this past week. Take time to discuss the answers and ask for responses. Additional verses are listed which will give you, the teacher, more insight. These lists are not exhaustive.

Feel free to pray and ask God for other verses that answer these questions for you. You can study these ahead of time and then either ask the students to look them up during class or just refer to them as you speak.

1. Have you accepted Jesus Christ as your Lord and Savior? Tell about that experience. (John 3:15-17, Rom. 3:22-24, 6:23, 10:9-10).

2. How has knowing Jesus changed your heart? (Rom. 12:2, 2 Cor. 3:18, Eph. 4:14- 15, Col. 3:15). **Answers will vary. May include: have become more loving, able to forgive, desire to seek Him, wanting God's way for my life, no longer living in sin, etc…**

3. This is your test on the definition of wisdom. Recite it out loud: "Wisdom is …"

4. Discuss any rules your parents gave you that you did not understand at the time. (Deut. 8:5-6, Gal. 3:21-26, 4:1-2, Heb. 12:5-11).

5. Is there a rule in the Old Testament about which you have wondered why God gave it? (Deut. 5:29, 8:6-7, Matt. 5:17-18, Rom. 7:12). **In Numbers 19:2-9, I wondered why God told the Israelites to kill a heifer and burn it and place it outside the camp. Whenever someone touched something unclean, they were to go and wash their hands in this cow's burned ashes. Then I read** *Little House on the Prairie*[5] **Antibacterial soap is make from lard (animal fat) and ashes. The Israelites did not know about germs, but God did! What seemed unreasonable was really God's protection.**

6. Look at the list of what God's Word accomplishes and explain how one of these is being accomplished in your life. (Ps. 19:7-11, 119:11, Rom. 12:2, Col. 3:16, James 1:21).

7. Why is it important to know Proverbs is a letter from a father's heart to his son? **When we look at it from this perspective it becomes less legalistic and our hearts are more open to receiving the instruction because we respect and love the Father Teacher.**

8. What good advice did you receive from your parents? Be specific.

9. Explain this comment: sins committed do not make you a sinner, but rather your sin nature makes you sin. (Rom. 6:7, 6:11-14, 7:4-6, 7:1 - 8:1-8, Eph. 2:1-10, 2:5). **Our sin nature is the disease. Our sins are the symptoms. We sin because we are sinners. Once the sin nature is taken care of through faith in Jesus, we can choose not to sin because the disease has been cured and the symptoms are no longer a direct result.**

10. If that statement is true, then why must you be born again and not just forgiven? (John 3:7, Rom. 3:20-28, 4:5, 6:20-22, 2 Cor. 5:17, Gal. 6:15, 1 John 1:9). **Forgiven means that no debt for our wrongs will be held against us, but only when we are born again do we have a new nature that is capable of choosing not to sin.**

11. Recite Proverbs 3:1-2.

Week 3
Week 3/Day 1: Acquiring Wisdom

In verses 20-23, is wisdom hiding and hard to find? **No**

In verses 24-29, is wisdom hard to find? **Yes**

Your reaction to wisdom makes the difference. This reminds me of a verse, Matthew 7:7.
What does this verse say you need to do to find Jesus, the All Wise One? **ask, seek, knock**

James 1:5 also says to ask for wisdom and it will be given to you. According to this verse to what extent will God give you wisdom? **generously**

"Shall live **securely** and will be at ease from the dread of evil." (Proverbs 1:33)

According to Proverbs 2:6 where does wisdom come from? **the Lord**

What are the consequences of not looking for wisdom? **wisdom will not answer in time of trouble, shall eat of fruit of own way, death, destruction**

Proverbs 2:1-5 again reminds you that you must look for wisdom. In verse 2 you must, "Make your ear **attentiv**" and "Incline your **heart**." Verse 3 says you must, "Cry for **discernment**, **lift** your voice for understanding." Verse 4 continues, "If you **seek** her." Then in verse 5, "You will discern the fear of the Lord and **discover** the knowledge of God."

1 Corinthians 1:18-31.

Write verse 25 here: **Because the foolishness of God is wiser than men, and the weakness of God is stronger than men.**

List 12 things from these verses that are yours if you seek wisdom.

1. **wisdom**
2. **knowledge**
3. **understanding**
4. **protection (shield)**
5. **our way preserved**
6. **discernment**
7. **righteousness**
8. **justice**
9. **equity**
10. **discretion**
11. **deliverance from evil**
12. **the land**

Questions to think about:

1. How does one seek wisdom? **By seeking first forgiveness through the blood of Jesus, thus being born again. Then through seeking God's wisdom through the reading and study of His word. Finally, by having a relationship with God through praise and prayer. (Seek, find, knock).**

2. Do you desire the results of wisdom you learned about today?

3. If your answer was "Yes", what step can you take today towards that end?

4. What blessings have you experienced because of your relationship with God?

5. Work on your memorization of Proverbs 3:1-3. (Add appropriate pictures or highlights.)

> My son, do not forget my __**teaching**__,
> But let your heart keep my __commandments__
> For length of __**days**__ and __**years**__ of life
> And __**peace**__ they will add to you.
> Do not let __**kindness**__ and __**truth**__ leave you;
> Bind them around your __**neck**__,
> Write them on the tablet of your __**heart**__.

Week 3/Day 2: Trusting God

In Acts 16:30, some jailers asked Paul and Silas, "What must I do to be saved?" Their reply was, "__**Believe**__ in the Lord Jesus, and you shall be saved."

Jesus, Himself, says, "I am the Way, the Truth, and the life; __**no one**__ comes to the Father except through me." (John 14:6).

In Jeremiah 29:11, God proclaims His intentions. "'For I know the plans I have for you;' declares, the Lord, 'plans for __**welfare**__ and not for calamity to give you a __**future**__ and a __**hope**__.'"

Can you think back to a time God was faithful in your life? It might have been before you even recognized Him or His Hand? _____ **Answers will vary**_____

See what blessings you can find in Proverbs 3:1-10. (I found 10.) What a good and mighty God we serve! **Length of days, years of life, peace, favor with God and man, good repute with God and man, God's directing, healing to body, refreshment to bones, filled barns, and full vats.**

Isaiah 30:15 helps me to center on resting and trusting in God. It shows how God's wisdom is different than man's wisdom. "In _____**repentance**_____ and _____**rest**_____ you will be saved, In _____**quietness**_____ and _____**trust**_____ is your strength."

Questions to think about:

1. Jesus' last words were, "It is finished." What things, other than Jesus' death and resurrection, are you trusting as part of your salvation? **Answers will vary, but might include church attendance, being good, doing good, tithing, forgiving others, etc.**

2. Do you seek God's blessings or a trusting relationship with God? **Answers will vary.**

3. In difficult times, which of the two choices in question two will see you through with your faith intact? **Seeking a trusting relationship with God.**

4. Have you been through a hard situation, prayed that God would change your circumstances, and found His answer to be no? Share that experience.

5. How was He still faithful in this?

6. Have you given your future to God?

7. Think about the verse Isaiah 30:15. This is actually a good definition of trust. Do you tend to rest and trust in a difficult situation or do you tend to worry and fret?

8. What does God say about worry? Look at Philippians 4: 6-7. **God commands us not to worry, but to praise Him, be thankful, and to pray about everything.**

9. Is worry sin? **Yes. God said not to be anxious. It is a lack of faith.**

10. Work on memorizing Proverbs 3:1-8.

Week 3/Day 3: Blessings and Curses

In verses 1, 6, 10, Why did God give the Israelites statutes and judgments? _____**So they would live and go in and take possession of the land, bring wisdom and understanding that other people will hear and say, "This great nation is a wise and understanding people," to fear God and teach their children.**

Read 4:11-20. Verses 15 and 19 contain two warnings. What are they? __**Watch yourselves carefully not to make graven image / beware not to worship sun or moon or stars.**__

Read 4:21-28. Verse 24 describes God as a _____**jealous**_____ God.

Moses gives the Israelites a warning in verses 25-28. They will be guilty of what sin? __**idolatry**__

What will be their punishment? __**Perish quickly from the land, be scattered among other nations.**__

What must you do to find God? __**Seek Him**__

Verse 30 prophesies that the people will return to God and will __**listen**__ to His voice.

Verse 31 states that your God is a compassionate God. What will He remember? __**His covenant**__

Verse 36 shows the compassion of God by reminding the Israelites of God's discipline. That discipline was to lead the Israelites to know the truth of verse 39. "The Lord, He is God in heaven above and on the earth below; __**there is no other**__."

Read Deuteronomy 4:40. What is the provision of verse 40? __**It will go well with you and your children, you may live long in the land that God is giving you for all time.**__

What condition must be met in order to gain these things? __**keep His statutes and commandments**__

Why do you think they chose these two verses as a part of such an important tradition?

__**Answers will vary. Believing in just one God was unique for that time and a foundational truth. To love Him and only Him and to teach their children would keep the faith pure. All other gods were nothing but wood with Satan behind the to keep God's children from following God.**__

What do these two verses mean to you? __**Answers will vary.**__

Verse 13 further explains God's requirements. What three things were the Israelites to do? __**fear only God, worship Him, swear by His name**__

If they upheld their end of the covenant, what did God promise? (vs. 18) __**It will be well with you, you may go in and possess the land.**__

Now turn over to chapter 11. This chapter further tells of the rewards of obedience. Notice God reminds the Israelites of His discipline in verse 2. Which of these verses remind you of the Shema? **vs. 1, 13, 18, 19, 20, 21**

List the curses that will come because of disobedience. (I found more than 30.)

the city	your produce	pestilence	sword
the country	your herd	consumption	blight
your basket	the young of flock	fever	mildew
your needing bowl	going out	inflammation	no rain
your offspring	coming in	fiery heart	no harvest
defeat	madness	adultery/rape	blindness
carcasses as food to birds	not live in house	boils	locusts
bewilderment	not use vineyard	tumors	oppression
Ox slaughtered – not eat	scabs	will be robbed	disease of Egypt
olive trees won't produce	worms	donkey stolen	failing of eyes
taken to other nation	become a horror to others		sickness
sheep given to enemies	sons and daughters given to others		despair
no harvest	crushed by others	crickets	
destruction	alien rise above you	serve enemies	cannibalism
hostility	plagues		
trembling heart	no rest		

And, lastly, look at Deuteronomy 30:1-3. What was the purpose of God's discipline? **to draw their hearts back to God**

Questions to think about:

1. Remember a time you were punished and are now glad that you received that punishment. Refer to Romans 8:38. **Answers will vary.**

2. Remember a time you were punished when you thought the punishment was unjustified or too harsh. **Answers will vary.**

3. Did you change your heart or actions in either one of the instances of #1 or #2?

4. Sometimes God is not punishing you but rather pruning you through the tough circumstances of life. How is pruning different than punishment? **Punishment is a direct result of sin or of not being**

in a close relationship to God. Pruning may feel like punishment, but its purpose is to mature us and to get rid of harmful attitudes, situations, or people in our lives so that we can grow healthy and more fruit.

5. Work on memorizing Proverbs 3:1-3. Begin adding verse 4.

> My ___**son**___ , do not forget my ___**teachings**___ ,
> But let your ___**heart**___ keep my ___**commandments**___ ;
> For ___**length**___ of ___**day**___ and ___**years**___ of life
> And _**peace**___ they will add to you.
> Do not let ___**kindness**___ and ___**truth**___ leave you;
> ___**Bind**___ them around your ___**neck**___ ,
> ___**write**___ them on the tablet of your ___**heart**___ .
> So you will find favor and good repute
> In the sight of God and man.

Week 3/Day 4: Choosing Wisdom

Read Proverbs 3:13-26. According to verse 14, whose profit is better than silver and whose gain is better than fine gold? ___**Wisdom's**___

Do you think the majority of people in today's world would agree with this statement? Why or why not? ___**No. Most people seek for gold and material goods.**___

What are your desires? ___**Answers will vary.**___

The 7 byproducts of seeking God are listed in Proverbs 3:16-18. List them below:

1. **long life**
2. **riches**
3. **honor**
4. **pleasant ways**
5. **peace**
6. **life**
7. **happiness**

"God's Word is ___**living**___ and ___**active**___ and sharper than any two-edged sword." (Heb. 4:12) We need to read it, memorize it, think about, pray through it, and read it again.

Read 2 Timothy 3:16-17. What four actions is Scripture profitable for?

1. **teaching**
2. **reproof**
3. **correction**
4. **training in righteousness**

What is the reason given for these actions in vs. 17? **so that man may be adequately equipped for every good work**

These men and women chose the narrow gate of Matthew 7:13-14. "Enter by the narrow gate, for the gate is wide and the way is broad that leads to **destruction**, and many are those who enter by it. For the gate is small and the way is narrow that leads to **life**, and few are those who find it."

Questions to think about:

1. In what ways have you decided to go God's direction rather than the world's?

2. How has God given you the strength to go against the flow?

3. Work on memorizing Proverbs 3:1-3.

My **son**, do not **forget** my **teaching**,
But let your **heart** **keep** my **commandments**;
For **length** of **days** and **years** of **life**
And **peace** they will **add** to you.
Do not let **kindness** and **truth** **leave** you;
Bind them **around** your **neck**,
Write them on the **tablet** of your **heart**.
So you will find **favor** and good **repute**
In sight of **God** and man.

Week 3/Day 5: Doing Good Deeds

Start with verse 27. "Do not withhold good from those to whom it is due, when it is in **your power** to do it."

Choose two people who you can do something special for just because it is in your power to do it.

Person 1:   Who?
              What?

Person 2:   Who?
              What?

1 Thessalonians 4:11 tells you to "Make it our ambition to lead a quiet life and attend to your **___own___** **business___** and work with **___your___ hands___**."

There is a right time to contend or confront another but not without cause. Proverbs 25:21-22 says, "If your enemy is hungry, **___give___ him___** food to eat; and if he is thirsty, **___give___ him___** water to drink; For you will heap burning coals on his head, and the Lord will **___reward___** you." God will reward your kindness. The heaping of coals on your enemy's head may lead him to seek forgiveness or restitution or at least make him be a bit nicer to you.

Questions to think about:

1. Tell about a time when you blessed someone anonymously.

2. Tell how you felt when you did something for someone else anonymously.

3. Tell how you feel when someone goes out of their way to do something nice for you.

4. Be ready to recite Proverbs 1:1-4.

Week 3 Group Discussion

The following questions were posed after the lessons this past week. Take time to discuss the answers and ask for responses. Additional verses are listed which will give you, the teacher, more insight. These lists are not exhaustive. Feel free to pray and ask God for other verses that answer these questions for you. You can study these ahead of time and then either ask the students to look them up during class or just refer to them as you speak.

1. Think about the verse Isaiah 30:15. This is actually a good definition of trust. Doyou tend to rest and trust in a difficult situation or do you tend to worry and fret? (Ps. 56:11, Matt.11:28-30).

2. Jesus' last words were, "It is finished." What things, other than Jesus' death and resurrection, do you try to make part of your salvation? (Phil. 3:7-11, Rom. 10:4, 11:6). **Answers may include being good, not cussing, going to church, pleasing others, tithing, witnessing, daily quiet time, etc...**

3. Do you seek God's blessings or a relationship with God? Why? (Rom. 8:15-16, Eph. 1:3-6).

4. What blessings have you experienced because of your relationship with God?

5. Sometimes God is not punishing you but rather pruning you through the tough circumstances of life. How is pruning different than punishment? (John 15:1-5, 2 Tim. 3:16-17). **Punishment is a direct consequence of sin. Pruning is training and teaching. They may feel the same as sometimes things are taken from us or we are not given what we want, but the motive is much different. We should confess sin and endure through pruning.**

6. In what ways have you decided to go God's direction rather than the world's? (Gal. 5:19-21, James 4:4, 1 John 2:15-16).

7. How has God given you the strength to go against the flow? (Ps. 28:7, Is. 30:15, 1 Cor. 10:14, 1 Peter 4:11).

8. Tell about a time when you blessed someone anonymously. (Luke 6:28, John 13:14-17, Romans 12:14).

9. Who did you surprise this week with a good deed? What did you do?

10. Recite Proverbs 3:1-4.

Week 4
Week 4/Day 1: Choices and Consequences

Fill out the following chart:

	ATTITUDE	OUTCOME	ATTITUDE	OUTCOME
vs. 32	crooked man	abomination	upright	intimacy with God
vs. 33	**wicked**	**curse of God**	**righteous**	**house blessed**
vs. 34	**scoffers**	**God scoffs at them**	**afflicted**	**grace**
vs. 35	**fools**	**dishonor**	**wise**	**honor**

His throne_____

In verse 8, the Word proclaims that God's judgment will be done in righteousness and with __**equity**_____. This means He will not play favorites. Each of us will be judged based upon whether we accepted Jesus Christ as our Savior.

Verse 10 is a promise you can stand on. Write this verse out below. __**And those who know Your name will put their trust in You. For You, O Lord, have not forsaken those who seek You.**__

_____

Proverbs 3:32: For the __**devious**__ man is an abomination to the Lord; But He is intimate with the __**upright**__.

I John 1:9. Write this verse out here: __**If we confess our sins, He is faithful and righteous to forgive us our sins and to cleanse us from all unrighteousness.**__

_____

Do you desire God's blessing, protection, provision, mercy, and love, or do you desire Him? _____When we desire God more than His blessings, we will receive His many blessings in abundance.

Proverbs 3:33 says, "The curse of the Lord is on the house of the __**wicked**__,

But He blesses the dwelling of the __**righteous**__."

Read Proverbs 10:1. This is a great verse to memorize. Are you are blessing or a curse in your home or with your family? _____We all are both sometimes.

Write about a time when you were a blessing: _____
_____

Write about a time when you were a curse: _____
_____

Questions to think about:

1. Which life is more real—this earthly one or your eternal one? Explain. **Both lives are equally real even though we can't see the spiritual realm that is right here around us. Our eternal home is more real in the sense that it will last forever and we will have imperishable bodies there.**

2. What riches should we seek? **Eternal riches stored for us up in heaven.**

3. How are God's curses used to bless? **They should make us see our sinfulness and make us turn to Him with repentance.**

4. In the Old Testament, was God angry and unforgiving or patient and faithful? **Only after God was patient and faithful for many centuries did He act upon His anger and refuse to take away the consequences of the Israelites' sins. However, even then, God gave them provision for returning to Him. He eventually gave us His final answer in the birth, death, and resurrection of Jesus Christ.**

5. Work on memorizing Proverbs 1:1-6. Add pictures to verses 5-6 in appendix A

Week 4/Day 2: Grace/Mercy, Honor/Dishonor

Paul, the great apostle of the New Testament cried out to God in his affliction three times (2 Cor. 12:7-10). God's response was not taking the affliction out of Paul's life, but rather, He replied, "My __grace__ is __sufficient__ for you."

What do your afflictions bring: grace or prideful independence? _____

Write the definition of wisdom from lesson one. __**The ability to judge correctly and use our knowledge to avoid trouble, solve problems, reach goals, and succeed in life based upon God's principles.**__

Are you having daily time reading God's Word? _____

Do you spend daily time in prayer speaking and listening? _____

Think of someone you honor and list five characteristics of that person.

Person: _____
1.
2.
3.
4.
5.

Think of someone you dishonor (or think badly of) and list five characteristics of that person.

Person: _____
1.
2.
3.
4.
5.

Which person acts wisely? _____

Which person displays foolish characteristics? _____

Questions to think about:

1. Describe the difference between grace and mercy and tell what they saved you from and to. **Grace is getting what we don't deserve. Grace gave us forgiveness and new life and a relationship with God. Mercy is not getting what we deserve. Mercy kept us from condemnation, death, and hell.**

2. Are you a woman of honor or dishonor?

3. What do you need to begin to be aware of and to practice to make you more honorable?

4. Practice reciting your memorized verses.

My son …

For length …

Do not let …

So you will …

Trust in the __**Lord**__ with all your __**heart**__

And do not ___**lean**___ on your own __**understanding**__

In all your _____**ways**_____ acknowledge Him,

And He will make your __**paths**_____ **straight**_____ .

Week 4/Day 3: Living Wisely

According to verse 5, what should you seek to own? _____**Wisdom and understanding**_____

Vs. 6 What will wisdom do if you don't forsake her but, rather, love her? __**She will guard me and watch over me.**__

Vs. 7 What is the beginning of wisdom? _____**to acquire wisdom**_____

Will wisdom by itself be enough? ____**No**____

What else will you need? ____**understanding**____

Vs. 8 If I prize wisdom what will I get? ____**She will exalt me and honor me.**____

Vs. 8-9 If I embrace her what will I get? ____**grace and crown of beauty**____ To be exalted means to be lifted up, to have a good reputation, to be honored.

According to vs. 10 what will it gain a son if he accepts these teachings from his father? __**more years of life**__

Vs. 13 How is wisdom gained? ____**Take hold of instruction and hang on!**____

Can an unbeliever be wise? (See 1 Cor.1 and 2.) __**no**__

Matthew 6:33 reemphasizes this concept: "But seek __**first**__ His kingdom and His righteousness; and all these things shall be added to you."

What must you acquire first? **The kingdom of God**

Each situation I turn over to God and refuse to worry about brings calm and peace rather than worry and turmoil. What situation or person do you need to practice praying about and refuse to worry about?

_____

_____

Questions to think about:

1. If an unbeliever cannot be truly wise, then is wisdom more about your actions here on earth or your future in heaven? **Our future in heaven, but eternity starts now!**

2. Jesus gives you wisdom to live this life and to prepare for eternity. How can wisdom prepare you for eternity? **By learning to live wisely now, your character is being formed that will allow you to be mature and fruitful in your heavenly tasks.**

3. Do you tend to worry?

4. What do you need to do when you are tempted to worry?

5. What is a worry concerning you right now you can give to God by thanking Him and asking Him to handle it?

6. Work on memorizing Proverbs 3:1-6.

    My son …
    For length …
    Do not let …
    So you will …

    Trust in the __**Lord**__ with all your __**heart**__
    And do not ____**lean**_____ on your own __**understanding**_____
    In all your _____**ways**___ acknowledge Him,
    And He will make your __**paths**_____ **straight**_____ .

Week 4/Day 4: Wisdom Found

Look up 1 Corinthian 2:12-14 and fill in the blanks.

"Now we have received, not the spirit of the __**world**_____ , but
the Spirit who is from __**God**_____ , so we may know the things
__**freely**_____ given to us by God, which things we also speak, not in
words taught by __**human**_____ wisdom, but those taught by the
__**Spirit**_____ , combining spiritual thought with spiritual words."

Who is your teacher?   __**The Holy Spirit**__

Behold, I long for Your precepts. (vs. 40)
I   **(Answers will vary)**
B
L
E

Questions to think about:

1. What does following God's Word mean in your life?

2. What changes do you need to make so God's Word is a priority in each day?

3. Work on your memory verses.

    My son …
    For length …
    Do not let …
    So you will …

    Trust in the ____**Lord**____ with all your __**heart**__
    And do not ____**lean**____ on your own __**understanding**__
    In all your ___**ways**___ ____**acknowledge**____ Him,
    And He will ___**make**___ your ___**paths**___ ___**straight**___.

Week 4/Day 5: Worldviews

What word is repeated in Isaiah 6:3? ___**Holy**___

What words are repeated in Revelation 19:16? ___**King, Lord**___

Write what Philippians 3:13-14 tells you to do. __**Forget what lies behind, reach forward to what lies ahead; press on**__

A world view answers eight questions. Write a brief answer to the following questions to summarize your world view. Remember to think big picture. (**Answers are from a Biblical world view.**)

1. Who are we? **We are created beings. Our Creator loves us and wants us to be in a loving relationship with Him.**

2. Where did we come from? **God created each of us uniquely and knew us before there was time.**

3. What does it mean to be human? **To be human is to have an eternal soul, the ability to reason, and the ability of language.**

4. Why am I here? **To love God and worship Him.**

5. What is wrong? **Adam and Eve sinned in the Garden of Eden bringing physical and spiritual death. We are separated from God in our natural, fallen state.**

6. What is the solution? Is there a God? **The sacrifice of Jesus Christ is the only answer. When we accept His sacrifice and choose to live for Him rather than for ourselves, we can again commune with God and look forward to heaven. There is one true, living God.**

7. Where are we going? **Men's souls are eternal and all men will spend that eternity in heaven or hell.**

8. How can we get there? **The only deciding factor on where we spend eternity is whether we have chosen to receive God's free gift of salvation through faith in Jesus or not.**

Questions to think about:

1. How often must you choose to not enter the path of the wicked?

2. How can you avoid even entering the path of wickedness?

3. What influences do you have in your life you must guard against so you won't enter the path of wickedness?

4. Keep memorizing.

    My son …
    For length …
    Do not let …
    So you will …

    Trust in the ___**Lord**___ with all your ___**heart**___
    And do not ___**lean**___ on your own ___**understanding**___
    In all your ___**ways**___ ___**acknowledge**___ Him,
    And He will ___**make**___ your ___**paths**___ ___**straight**___.

Week 4 Group Discussion

The following questions were posed after the lessons this past week. Take time to discuss the answers and ask for responses. Additional verses are listed which will give you, the teacher, more insight. These lists are not exhaustive. Feel free to pray and ask God for other verses that answer these questions for you. You can study these ahead of time and then either ask the students to look them up during class or just refer to them as you speak.

1. Which life is more real—this earthly one or your eternal one? Explain. (Mark 2:5-11, John 14:1-6, 17:3, Rev. 20:11-15, 21:1-7, 16-27, 22:1-6). **They are both equally real and valid. However, the spiritual life may be said to be more real because it is eternal and will not pass away. The spiritual realm exists all around us even though we can't see it. 2 Kings 6:16-17.**

2. How are God's curses used to bless you? (Deut. 6, 8, 27, 28, 30:1-3, 15-20, 1 John 1:9). **Curses and blessings in the Old Testament were part of the Mosaic Law and had to do with the Israelites' earthly existence. Under the New Testament covenant, blessings are usually given in eternity. There is not such a direct link between the blessings and curses and your behavior as there was in the OT. That being said, God does still bless us at times, because He loves us. But we are promised troubles and tribulations in this world. You must discern whether a trial is upon us because of sin (natural consequences and discipline), pruning (John 15:2), or just because you reside in Satan's domain—the world. The Holy spirit convicts you of your sins, so you might despise them and turn back to God.**

3. Describe the difference between grace and mercy and tell what they saved you from and to. (Is. 63:8-9, Luke 1:77-79, Rom. 5:20-21, 9:15, 2 Cor. 12:9, Eph. 2:8, 2:4-7, Titus 3:7, Heb. 4:16, James 4:6) **Mercy: not given what you deserve—saves you from death and judgment. Grace: given what you don't deserve—salvation, forgiveness, love, adoption, etc.**

4. If an unbeliever cannot be truly wise, then is wisdom more about your actions here on earth or your future in heaven? (1 Cor. 1:18-31, 2:1-16) **Both. God's Spirit speaks to His children spiritual wisdom so you might make right and holy choices on this earth. Making these right decisions and choosing to live in purity and holiness prepares you for your future in heaven.**

5. Jesus gives you wisdom to live this life and to prepare for eternity. How can wisdom prepare you for eternity? (1 Cor. 6:2-3) **God is maturing His saints to ride with Him in the final battle and to judge nations and angels. Using wisdom now, prepares us for these challenges ahead.**

6. What does following God's Word mean in your life? (Col. 3:16, 1 Thess. 2:13, 2 Tim. 3:16, James 1:21). **Answers will vary but may include: It's just a list of do's and don't's; I read it when I am**

in a bind, Following His moral law; legalism; seeking God through His word so that I can have a relationship with Him.

7. How often must you choose to not enter the path of the wicked? (Rom. 6:1-2, 11-18, 13:14, 18:5-6). **Constantly. It is all around us. If we step one foot into a raging river, we can be swept away. We must be always watchful and diligent to recognize and refute evil.**

8. How can you avoid even entering the path of wickedness? What influences do you have in your life you must guard against so you won't enter the path of wickedness? **Answers will vary but may include: Don't go places that tempt me. Don't be around people that tempt me. Guarding my thought life. Being around people who are Christians and choose well what activities and conversation they partake in.**

9. Answer the worldview questions with biblical answers. **See answers in lesson.**

10. Is worry acceptable for a Christian or is it sin? (Prov. 3:5-6, Matt. 6:25, 6:34, Luke 12:25, Phil. 4:6-7, 1 Peter 5:6-7) **Christians are commanded not to worry, but rather to pray and trust God thanking Him ahead of time for His answers, therefore, worry is a sin. It is a symptom of not trusting.**

11. Recite Proverbs 3:1-6.

Week 5
Week 5/Day 1: Guarding Your Heart

To lead such a life is not easy and requires constant guarding. Read Proverbs 4:23: "__**Watch**____ over your heart with all __**diligence**_____, for from it flows the springs of life."

How do you guard your heart? Write out 2 Corinthians 10:5: __**We are destroying speculations and every lofty thing raised up against the knowledge of God, and we are taking every thought captive to the obedience of Christ.**_____

Write out Proverbs 16:9 __**The mind of a man plans his way, But the Lord directs his steps.**

Write out in the space below where you feel, and prayerfully have considered, is the direction God is leading you. Examples: to a daily quiet time, to a more respectful attitude toward siblings, to become a more motivated student or worker, to develop my skills with younger children, computers, etc.

Try to list at least 3.

1.
2.
3.

Questions to think about:

1. What thoughts has Satan put into your mind that you have chosen to believe? **Answers will vary but may include: "I am no good." "I am unworthy." "I won't ever amount to anything." "I don't deserve to be loved." "I am only worthy if other people approve of me." "I am only worthy when I achieve something." Etc.**

2. How can you tell if a thought is your own, Satan's, or God's? **See if it lines up with Scripture or not.**

3. Explain Archbishop Leighton's quote and apply to your own life. **It is important to have a purpose, know that purpose, and work towards that purpose. I need to make sure that my every effort is in line with my purpose and prioritize my time and my activities to this purpose. As a Christian my purpose should include glorifying God and loving Him forever.**

4. Work on your memorization of Proverbs 3:1-7.

    My son …
    For length …

Do not let …
So you will …
Trust in the …
And do not …
In all your …
And He will …

Do not be __**wise**__ in your own _____**eyes**_____,
__**Fear**__ the Lord and _____**turn** **away**_____ from ____**evil**____.

Week 5/Day 2: The Pleasure of Sin

Read Hebrews 11:25-26. "Choosing rather to endure ill-treatment with the people of God than to enjoy the __ **passing** **pleasures** **of** **sin**___, considering the reproach of Christ greater riches than the treasures of Egypt; for he was looking to the reward."

But look at Proverbs 5:4, "In the end she is as bitter as ___**wormwood**___, Sharp as a two-edged sword." Verse 5 continues by saying that she leads to __**death**___.

Look up Romans 14:11, Philippians 2:10, and Isaiah 45:23-24. When sin entices you, what should you remember? ____**We must bow before Jesus and give account.**_____

Questions to think about:

1. When sin entices you what should you remember? **The pleasures of sin are passing and you will left with regret and guilt and death.**

2. What sin do you have a tendency towards or had a tendency towards in the past?

3. How is it more rewarding to choose not to commit this sin rather to give in to it.

4. What are the rewards? **Free conscience, relationship with God, peace, feeling good about myself, knowing the power of Jesus to overcome.**

5. Work on memory verses Proverbs 3:1-7 and add verse 8 to your appendix C.

Week 5/Day3: Contentment

Proverbs 19:20 says, "Listen to ____**counsel**____ and accept __**discipline**____, That you may be wise the rest of your days."

And Proverbs 15:22 says, "Without consultation, plans are __**frustrated**__,
But with many counselors they succeed."

Most marriages do well in two areas and struggle in the third. Which two are you good at?
Which one do you need to work on? _____

List things you tend to covet.

1.
2.
3.
4.
5.

What are some steps you can take to flee from temptation?

1.
2.
3.
4.
5.

Try to list 20 things for which you are grateful to God.

Lastly, Proverbs 5:21 should help you keep within moral boundaries. "For the ways of ____**man**____ are before the eyes of the __**Lord**___, and He watches all his paths."

Questions to think about:

1. Are you content in your present relationship status?

2. What commitment or renewal of a commitment do you need to make?

3. What type of things do you covet?

4. Were you able to come up with 20 things you are grateful for?

5. Practice reciting Proverbs 3:1-8.

> My son …
> For length …

Do not let …
So you will …
Trust in the …
And do not …
In all your …
And He will …
Do not be ___**wise**___ in your own ___**eyes**___,
___**Fear**___ the Lord and ___**turn**___ ___**away**___ from ___**evil**___.
It will be ___**healing**___ to your body
And ___**refreshment**___ to your bones.

Week 5/Day 4: Surety and Pledges

Read James 3:2-12.
Have you been guilty of sins of the tongue? _____

Write out Romans 12:18: ___**If possible, so far as it depends on you, be at peace with all men.**___

_____

Questions to think about:

1. Why, do you think, God is against surety? God **holds each of us accountable for our own debts and responsibilities.**

2. How is a half-truth a whole lie? **A lie is anything that does not represent the whole truth. The intent of a half-truth is to deceive.**

3. What sins of the tongue do you struggle with?

4. Why does it seem easier to ask for God's forgiveness than man's? **God's forgiveness is assured to the believer; man's is not.**

5. What do you base your self-esteem on—how you look, what you do, others' opinions about you, or that you are God's beloved child?

6. Recite to someone Proverbs 3:1-8.

7. Here's some clues for your two newest verses: 7 and 8.

    Do not be ___**wise**___ in your own ___**eyes**___,
    ___**Fear**___ the Lord and ___**turn**___ ___**away**___ from ___**evil**___.

It will be __**healing**__ to your body
And __**refreshment**__ to your bones.

Week 5/Day 5: Industry vs. Idleness

What will, "A little sleep, a little slumber, a little folding of the hands to rest," lead to? __**poverty**__

List the work God would have you to do. Work may include an occupation, taking care of children, ministry, yard work, house work, volunteer work, etc.

"According to the grace of God which was given to me, like a wise master builder I laid a foundation, and another is building on it. But each man must be careful how he builds on it. For no man can lay a foundation other than the one which is laid, which is Jesus Christ. Now if any man builds on the foundation with gold, silver, precious stones, wood, hay, straw, each man's work __**will become evident**__; for the day will show it because it is to be revealed with fire, and the fire itself will test the __**quality**__ of each man's work. If any man's work which he has built on it remains, he will receive a reward. If any man's work is burned up, he will suffer loss; but he himself will be saved, yet so as __**through fire**__."

How will your life's work stand the test of fire? Are you working for approval or working out of obedience?

Questions to think about:

1. Why is work good for your physical health? Your mental health? Your emotional health? **Physical work keeps your body fit and trim giving you energy and releasing endorphins which make you feel satisfied and happy. Work helps you to feel useful and needed.**

2. What type of work do you like to do best?

3. Fill in the blanks for Proverbs 3:1-8.

My son, do not __**forget**__ my __**teaching**__,
But let your __**heart**__ keep my __**commandments**__;
For __**length**__ of __**days**__ and __**years**__ of ___life___
And __**peace**__ they will __**add**__ to you.
Do not let __**kindness**__ and __**truth**__ leave you;
__**Bind**__ them around your neck,
__**Write**__ them on the __**tablet**__ of your __**heart**__,

So you will find ____**favor**____ and good ____**repute**____

In the ____**sight**____ of ____**God**____ and ____**man**_____.

____Trust_____ in the __**Lord**____ with all ____**your**____ **heart**____ .

And do not ____**lean**____ on you own ____**understanding**____ ,

In ____**all**____ your ways __**acknowledge**____ Him,

And He will make your ____**paths**____ **straight**____ .

Do not be ____**wise**____ in your own eyes;

Fear the ____**Lord**____ and ____**turn**____ away from evil.

It will be ____**healing**____ to your body

And ____**refreshment**____ to your bones.

Week 5 Group Discussion

The following questions were posed after the lessons this past week. Take time to discuss the answers and ask for responses. Additional verses are listed which will give you, the teacher, more insight. These lists are not exhaustive. Feel free to pray and ask God for other verses that answer these questions for you. You can study these ahead of time and then either ask the students to look them up during class or just refer to them as you speak.

1. What lies has Satan put into your mind that you have chosen to believe? (John 8:44, Rom. 1:25, 2 Cor. 10:3-5) **Answers will vary, but may include: I am ugly; I'll never be good enough; I am unlovable; I need others to love me; I will never measure up to what others expect of me; If I have money, I can't be a good Christian; etc…**

2. When you recognize a lie you have been believing, how can you combat it?(Matt. 4:4, 7, 10, 2 Cor. 10:5) **You do this by finding a truth in God's word and speaking this truth against Satan.**

3. Explain Archbishop Leighton's quote and apply to your own life. ("To him that knoweth not the port to which he is bound, no wind is favorable. He may be well equipped, a good craft, sails set, ballast right, cargo well packed; but he wants somewhere to go, a port to enter. All his activity and preparation are useless without a purpose."[28] (Heb. 6:19, 10:23, 1 Cor. 9:24-27) **I may doing everything *right*, have all the *right* friends, *right* lifestyle, but without direction, I will just flounder and never know real peace. As a Christian, I may be going to church, practicing love and patience, tithing, etc…, but unless I know where I am going (a deeper walk with God), it won't gain me the peace that I seek.**

4. When sin entices you what should you remember? (John 14:6, Rom. 3:23, Col. 3:6-15, John 2:1, 2:16, 2:21, 2:28, 3:4-8, 4:4) **God's way is better in the long run. Sin will break my relationship with God. Jesus died for my sins. I don't want to hurt Him by adding more sins to His burden. Sin leads to death. The righteous will inherit eternal life. Etc…**

5. How is it more rewarding to choose not to commit this sin rather to give in to it. What are the rewards? (John 15:10-11, 1 John 3:21) **Renewed relationship with God the Father, strengthening of your discerning of the Holy Spirit's conviction, no guilt feelings, confidence before God, and a pure and sincere heart.**

6. What type of things do you covet? (Luke 3:14, 2 Cor. 12:10, Phil. 4:11, Heb.13:5, James 4:1-3).

7. How can you remember your blessings and why is this important? (Eph. 1:3-8, James 1:17). **Remembering our blessings will help us to stay focused on what all we do have and help us to be content and uncomplaining. It will change our point of view and help us to act wisely.**

8. How is a half-truth a whole lie? (1 John 2:21). **A lie is anything said or not said with the intention of deception. By not telling the whole truth, one is trying to deceive and get by with something.**

9. Recite aloud Proverbs 3:1-8.

10. Share drawings from day 4.

Week 6
Week 6/Day 1: Foolish Behaviors

Write out 2 Corinthians 10:5. <u>**We are destroying speculations and every lofty thing raised up against the knowledge of God, and we are taking every thought captive to the obedience of Christ.**</u>

Put a star by any of the following foolish actions you sometimes get caught doing. Begin to pray now that God will help you catch yourself the next time you do this and choose to repent and give a blessing instead.

gossip   cursing   cussing   criticism   belittling   lying

sneering   making fun   spreading strife   winking of the eye

signaling with the feet   pointing with the fingers (literally or in your mind)

haughty eyes

Questions to think about:

1. Are your words to others bringing life or death?

2. How is half a truth a whole lie? **A lie is any misinformation of the truth meant to deceive.**

3. Which of these sins has become a habit for you?

4. Are you going to commit to not doing that which is an abomination to God?

5. Add Proverbs 5:9 and 10 to your Appendix C.

Week 6/Day 2: Discipline vs. Punishment

2 Timothy 3:16 reminds you that the Bible is the instruction manual for life and is profitable for what four things?

1. **Teaching**
2. **Reproof**
3. **Correction**
4. **Training in righteousness**

One more word on the benefits of discipline. Look at 2 Timothy 2:3-6. What three careers are compared to your Christian walk?

1. **Soldier**
2. **Athlete**
3. **Farmer**

Write verse 27 here: ___**Can a man take fire in his bosom and his clothes not be burned?**___

What is your answer to this question? ___**No**___

Can a man ignore discipline and not suffer the bad consequences? ___**No**___

Questions to think about:

1. How is being a Christian like a soldier? **He separates himself from the world to focus fully on his job seeking to please his commander.**

2. How is being a Christian like an athlete? **He competes according to the rules(God's rules as written in the Bible).**

3. How is being a Christian like a farmer? **He should be the first to receive hisShare of the crops (heavenly rewards).**

4. Which of these metaphors challenges you the most?

5. Recite Proverbs 3:1-10 aloud.

> My son, do not ___**forget**___ my ___**teaching**___,
> But let your ___**heart**___ keep my ___**commandments**___;
> For ___**length**___ of ___**days**___ and ___**years**___ of ___**life**___
> And ___**peace**___ they will ___**bring**___ to you.
> Do not let ___**kindness**___ and ___**truth**___ leave you;
> ___**Bind**___ them around your neck,
> ___**Write**___ them on the ___**tablet**___ of your ___**heart**___,
> So you will find ___**favor**___ and good ___**repute**___
> In the ___**sight**___ of ___**God**___ and ___**man**___.
> ___**Trust**___ in th ___**Lord**___ with all ___your ___**heart**___.
> And do not ___**lean**___ on you own ___**understanding**___,
> In ___**all**___ your ways ___**acknowledge**___ Him,

And He will make your ___**paths**___ ___**straight**___.
Do not be ___**wise**___ in your own eyes;
Fear the ___**Lord**___ and ___**turn**___ away from evil.
It will be ___**healing**___ to your body
And ___**refreshment**___ to your bones.
Honor the Lord from your ___**wealth**___
And from the first of all your ___**produce**___;
So your barns will be filled with ___**plenty**___
And your vats will overflow with ___**new wine**___.

Week 6/Day 3: Lust, Sin, Death

In Proverbs 6:25 where does the lie begin? ___**heart**___

James 1:14-15 holds the key. Write these verses out here. ___**But each one is tempted when he is carried away and enticed by his own lust. Then when lust has conceived, it gives birth to sin; and when sin is accomplished, it brings forth death.**___

Turn to 1 John 2:15-16 and fill in the blanks.

"Do not love the ___**world**___ nor the things in the ___**world**___.
If anyone loves the ___**world**___, the love of the Father is not in him. For all that is in the ___ **world**___, the lust of the ___**flesh**___ and the lust of the ___**eyes**___ and the boastful ___**pride**___ of life, is not from the Father, but is from the ___**world**___."

You are tempted by what you see, what you desire, what you think will fulfill and bring power. But you are to be in the world, but not of the world (John 15:19).
1 John 2:17 goes on to state, "The ___**world**___ is passing away, also its ___**lusts**___; but the one who does the will of God lives forever."

According to this verse what should you focus on? Things that are . . .

1. **True**
2. **Honorable**
3. **Right**
4. **Pure**
5. **Lovely**
6. **of Good Repute**
7. **Excellent**
8. **Worthy of Praise**

"Now flee from youthful_____**lusts**_____ and pursue righteousness, faith, love and peace, with those who call on the Lord from a pure heart."
(2 Timothy 2:22).

Questions to think about:

1. Try to not think of the number 7.

2. Seven is probably all you can think about. Now think about the number 21. Are thinking about 7 anymore?

3. Your mind can only think on one thing at a time. When you are tempted by the things of this world, what verse of Scripture can you meditate on to keep your mind focused on God.

4. Practice your memory verses through vs. 10.

> My son …
> But let your …
> For …
> And …
> Do not let …
> Bind …
> Write …
> So you will …
> In the …
> Trust …
> And do not …
> In all …
> And He …
> Do not be …
> Fear …
> It will be …
> And …
> Honor the Lord from your ___**wealth**_____
> And from the first of all your ___**produce**_____;
> So your barns will be filled with ___**plenty**_____
> And your vats will overflow with ___**new**_____**wine**_____.

Week 6/Day 4: Leaving Sin Behind

1 John 1:8 says "If we say we have __**no**_____**sin**_____, we are deceiving ourselves, and the ____**truth**_____is not in us."

Thus 1 John 1:9 says, "If we confess _____**our**_____**sins**_____, He is faithful and righteous to forgive us our sins and cleanse us from all unrighteousness."

Romans 8:1 is a great verse to memorize. "Therefore there is now ____**no**_____ ____**condemnation**_____ for those who are in Christ Jesus."

What nature has God redeemed in you? ____**Your sin nature**_____

Does that mean you will never sin again? ____**no**_____

When you do mess up, what are you to do? _____**confess**_____

Questions to think about:

1. If you are born again, you are no longer a caterpillar, but a butterfly. Are you soaring in the clouds or still trying to get up off the ground?

2. Why should you who are forgiven from your sins, no longer live in sin? **Sin separates the Christian from the fellowship with God. Living in sin will keep the Christian from knowing God deeper and hearing His voice. Continuing to live in sin shows that your heart was not truthful when you asked Jesus to take control of your life. Are you truly saved? Living in sin has dire consequences and the protection and provision of God is withdrawn. Also others are watching and you are giving the Kingdom of God a bad name possibly keeping others from knowing God's saving grace through Jesus.**

3. God is like a father, only perfect. This makes you His son or daughter. How does God respond to His children's sin? **He wants us to come to Him with confession and repentance sorry for having done something that was not right. Then He wants to pull up into His lap and give us a big hug!**

4. Say your memory verses Proverbs 3:1-10.

   My son …
   But let your …
   For …
   And …
   Do not let …
   Bind …

Write …

So you will …

In the …

Trust …

And do not …

In all …

And He …

Do not be …

Fear …

It will be …

And …

Honor the **Lord** from your **wealth**

And from the **first** of all your **produce** ;

So your **barns** will be filled with **plenty**

And your **vats** will overflow with **new wine** .

Week 6/Day 5: Who is Wisdom?

Who is wisdom? **Jesus** Still not sure?

Sound familiar? Try John 14:6, "**Jesus** said to him, 'I am the Way, the Truth, and the Life; no one comes to the Father but through Me.'"

Look at I Corinthians 1:30. "But by His doing you are in Christ Jesus, who became to us **wisdom** from God, and righteousness and sanctification, and redemption."

Jesus was with God in the beginning **Answers will vary John 1:1, 1 John 1:1-3**

Righteousness is His. **Matt. 3:15, Rom. 3:25, Rom. 5:18, Rom. 10:4, 1 Cor. 1:30**

Power is His. **Matt. 9:6, Matt. 24:30, Matt. 28:18, Rom. 1:1, 4, 1 Cor. 1:24**

Those who seek Him find Him. **Matt. 6:33, Matt. 7:7, Luke 11:9, Col. 3:1, Heb. 11:6**

Wealth is His. **Luke 16:11, Rom. 9:23, Rom. 11:33, Eph. 1:7, Eph. 1:18, Eph. 2:7**

His mouth will utter truth. **Matt. 14:33, Matt. 22:16, Mark 12:14, John 1:14, John 1:17, John 8:32**

He wants to endow those who love Him with wealth, to fill their treasuries. **Col. 2:2-3**

Blessed are those who keep His ways. <u>**Acts 2:28, 1 Cor. 4:17, Rev. 15:3**</u>

Those who hate Him love death. <u>**Rom. 6:21, John 15:18-25, Rom. 1:28-32**</u>

Those who find Him find life. <u>**Matt. 10:39, Matt 16:25**</u>

Questions to think about:

1. Write about a time when the character of Jesus showed you wisdom through a situation.

2. Say Proverbs 3:1-10.

> My son …
> But let your …
> Or …
> And …
> Do not let …
> Bind …
> Write …
> So you will …
> In the …
> Trust …
> And do not …
> In all …
> And He …
> Do not be …
> Fear …
> It will be …
> And …
> Honor …
> And from …
> So your …
> And your …

Week 6 Group Discussion.

The following questions were posed after the lessons this past week. Take time to discuss the answers and ask for responses. Additional verses are listed which will give you, the teacher, more insight. These lists are not exhaustive. Feel free to pray and ask God for other verses that answer these questions for you. You can study these ahead of time and then either ask the students to look them up during class or just refer to them as you speak.

1. Are your words bringing life or death to others? (Prov. 15:1, 18:21, 21:23, 25:11).

2. How is being a Christian like a soldier? An athlete? A farmer? (, Is. 28:24-29, 1Cor. 9:24-27, 2 Tim. 2:3-6, 4:7, James 5:7). **A soldier and a Christian must train diligently and be ready at all times for an attack from the enemy. They both must follow the commands of those of higher rank. They must put away things that would hinder them in their lives as a soldier and as a Christian. An athlete and a Christian both must train diligently. They play to win, and reaching the goal is their objective where they will be rewarded for the contest. A farmer and a Christian must both plant seeds that they may never see grow. If they are able to watch the growth, it is through faith that the growth will occur. They must both be patient and while not seeing the results of their labor, they must believe that the reward is coming—a harvest will occur. They must both know the sign of the times and know when to sow and when to reap. They must be diligent and ready to sow when the time comes and be able to distinguish between the wheat and the tares (truth and lies, faithful and unfaithful).**

3. Which of these metaphors challenges you the most?

4. Your mind can only think on one thing at a time. When you are tempted by the things of this world, share a verse of Scripture you can meditate on to keep your mind focused on God? (Rom. 12:2, Phil. 4:8, Col. 3:2).

5. If you are born again, you are no longer a caterpillar, but a butterfly. Are you soaring in the clouds or still trying to get up off the ground? What is the means to getting launched? (1 John 3:16, Matt. 4:17). **If you are a Christian but seem unable to soar above life's circumstances, you must know the truth and begin to walk in that truth putting aside the deeds of the flesh. Through Bible study and prayer, you must establish a relationship with God and accept His forgiveness and love as well as forgive those who have hurt you.**

6. Why should you who are forgiven from your sins, no longer live in sin? (John 8:11, Rom. 6:1-7, 6:22, Gal. 5:22). **Sin is a chain that will keep you from experiencing the victory and abundance that God has for you. Sin will keep you separated from a loving relationship with God the Father and Jesus the Son. Sin will deceive your mind and contort your views. You must choose not to be conformed to this world, but rather to renew your mind through the Word of God (Rom. 12:2). Sin will keep you in a place of punishment and self-reprisal rather than allowing you to accept God's view of compassion and love for you.**

7. God is like a father, only perfect. This makes you His son or daughter. How does God respond to His children's sin? (Psalm 103:8-14, Matthew 23:37, Mark 3:5, 11:15). **He is mindful that we are but dust and has great compassion on us. Sin does not make you no longer a son or daughter,**

but it keeps you from realizing the blessings of that relationship. God wants to gather us to Himself and protect us. He wants to heal us and comfort us. But God must judge sin in our lives. He must chase out the sins that bind us and keep us from Himself. He is quick to forgive and compassionate towards those who repent.

8. Share a time when the character of Jesus showed you wisdom through a situation.

9. Recite Proverbs 3:1-14 aloud.

Week 7
Week 7/Day 1: Renewing Your Mind

According to Ephesians 4:17-19 how did the Gentiles walk? __**futility of their mind, darkened in under-standing, excluded from life of God**__

They were "Being darkened in their understanding, excluded from the life of God because of the ignorance that is in them, because of the hardness of their heart; and they, having become __**callous**__ have given themselves over to sensuality for the practice of every kind of impurity with greediness."

And in Romans 1:21-25, people knew God, but did not __**honor**__ Him or give Him __**thanks**__. "And their foolish hearts were __**darkened**__. Professing to be wise, they became __**fools**__."

1 Corinthians 2:14 says, "A natural man does not accept the things of the Spirit of God, for they are __**foolishness**__ to him, he cannot understand them because they are spiritually appraised."

Are you still accepting Satan's accusations for sins you committed before you accepted Jesus as your Savior? ___

Look at Proverbs 8:32-34. According to these verses you must do 7 things. What are they?

1. **Listen**
2. **Keep God's ways**
3. **Heed instruction**
4. **Be wise**
5. **Do not neglect God's ways**
6. **Watch daily**
7. **Wait**

Questions to think about:

1. If someone chooses not to believe in the truth of the Bible does this make the Bible not true? **No. Truth stands on its own regardless of what man believes. What was, was.**

2. Are there absolute truths? **Absolutely. These are the truths based upon the unchanging character of God and His plans and promises.**

3. Name some of these absolute truths.

In the beginning God created.

When I was a sinner, Christ died for me.

If I confess with my mouth the Lord Jesus and believe in my heart that God raised Jesus from the dead, I will be saved.

God no longer condemns or judges me because Jesus took my blame.

I am God's adopted child and His heir and can look forward to heaven.

God hears my prayers.

God cares for me.

God has given us the Spirit of power, love, and a sound mind.

We are alive with God, forgiven, and no longer do we owe anything to God.

We can have all the wealth that comes from the full assurance of understanding.

We can know the truth about Jesus and God and in them get wisdom and knowledge.

God is still working in me to make me perfect and mature.

We can know God, the power of Jesus' resurrection, the fellowship of His suffering, and will be resurrected from the dead!

4. How can you "take every thought captive to the obedience of Christ"? **I must first slow down my thoughts and pay attention to them. This gets easier with practice. Then I must ask myself if that thought is true according to God's word. If it is I hold it tight. If it is not, then I must find the truth to refute it and tell Satan that he has no power over me because I am God's child. If the thought is coming from the world or from my own mind or recordings from the past, I must admit that they are lies and replace them with truth.**

5. Add Proverbs 3:11 to your Appendix C.

Week 7/Day 2: Wise Words

Prudence	Discretion	Righteous	Power
Noble things	Hates evil	Knowledge	Justice
Right things	Hates pride	Understanding	Love
Truthful	Sound counsel	Jewels	Riches
Honor	Wealth	Generous	

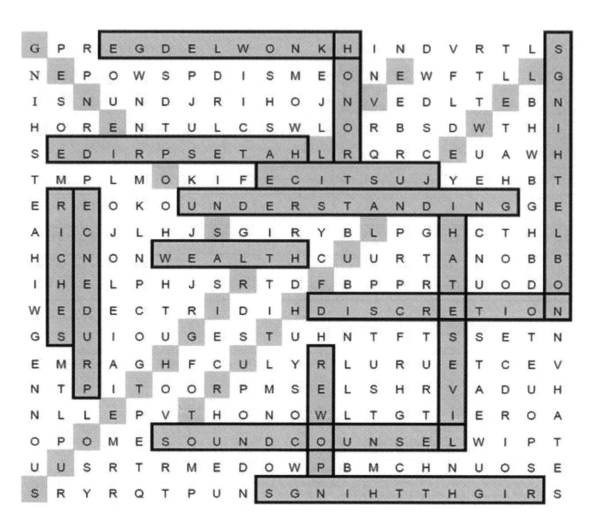

Questions to think about:

1. Add characteristics and results of wisdom from chapter 8 to your charts. (I found 19).

2. Start memorizing Proverbs 3:11.

My son, do not reject the ___**discipline**___ of the ____**Lord**____
Or __**loathe**_____ His __**reproof**___.

Week 7/Day 3: God's Inspired Words

Write these verses: ___**As a result we are no longer to be children, tossed here and there by waves and carried about by every wind of doctrine, by the trickery of men, by craftiness in deceitful scheming; but speaking truth in love, we are to grow up in all aspects into Him who is the head, even Christ.**___

Read 2 Timothy 3:16-17. What are the four things Paul tells Timothy that Scripture is profitable for? I know you have already studied this, but this is really important.

1. **Teaching**
2. **Reproof**
3. **Correction**
4. **Training in Righteousness**

How important is it, then, that you study Scripture diligently and deliberately? See 2 Timothy 3:14-15. __**Very important, so that we can have wisdom that leads to salvation through faith in Jesus.**__

Questions to think about:

1. What are you doing now that you think God is using to equip you for some future work?

2. What can you do to make Bible study more a part of every day?

3. Do you seek the Holy Spirit's wisdom before speaking the truth in love?

4. Why is this important?

5. Work on your memory verses.

> My son ...
> But let your ...
> For ...
> And ...
> Do not let ...
> Bind ...
> Write ...
> So you will ...
> In the ...
> Trust ...
> And do not ...
> In all ...
> And He ...
> Do not be ...
> Fear ...
> It will be ...

And …
Honor …
And from …
So your …
And your …
My son, do not ____**reject**____ the ____**discipline**____ of the Lord
Or __**loathe**__ His reproof.

Week 7/Day 4: Wisdom vs. Foolishness

	Wise Woman	Foolish Woman
Character:	established	boisterous / naïve–knowing nothing
Placement:	tops of heights of city	doorway of house
Calls to whom:	naïve/him who lacks understanding	those who pass by who are making their ways straight
Message:	Come, eat food, drink wine	Stolen water is sweet, bread eaten in secret is pleasant
Offers:	life, understanding	death

Questions to think about:

1. Why does the foolish woman look to trap the righteous and not the foolish? **The foolish already belong to the kingdom of Satan; they do not need to be lured there.**

2. Does Satan attack unbelievers or believers more? Why? **Believers. He wants to draw their hearts away from God so that they are ineffectual in the Kingdom of God.**

3. Almost there. Say Proverbs 3:1-11 by memory.

    My son …
    But let your …
    For …
    And …
    Do not let …
    Bind …
    Write …

So you will …
In the …
Trust …
And do not …
In all …
And He …
Do not be …
Fear …
It will be …
And …
Honor …
And from …
So your …
And your …
My son, do not ____**reject**____ the ___**discipline**___ of the ___**Lord**___
Or ___**loathe**___ His ___**reproof**_____.

Week 7/Day 5: Repent and Turn

Read Proverbs 9:7-9 and evaluate how you receive reproof. Do you listen and heed discipline or do you scoff at authority figures (including your husband)? _____

Do you turn and tell tales out of anger and resentment about the one who meted out the punishment or do you humble your heart and ask for forgiveness? _____
_____

Turn to Hebrews 12:4-13. Who does a father discipline? __**the son whom he loves**_____

According to Hebrews 12:6, what is God's motive for discipline? _____**love**_____
If God does not discipline you, according to Hebrews 12:8, what are you? ___**illegitimate**_____

According to Hebrews 12:9, what should your reaction to the one who disciplines you be? _____**respect**

According to Hebrews 12:10, what is God's motive for disciplining us? ___**our good and to share his Holiness**_____

Is discipline joyful at the moment? _____**no**_____

What does one trained by discipline bear in Hebrews 12:11? ___**graceful fruit of righteousness**__

What road have you been likely to take? _____

Are you willing to choose wisdom the next time discipline enters your life whether by human authority or God?

_____

Back to Proverbs 9—the litmus test is verses 8 and 9. Do you hate him who disciplines you or do you love him?

_____

Questions to think about:

1. When you were little and knew you had done something you shouldn't have done, did you fear your mom or dad?

2. When you drive over the speed limit do you fear the policeman sitting on the corner?

3. When you sin, do you fear God? **See 1 Peter 1:17-19.**

4. Recite Proverbs 3:1-11.

    > My son …
    > But let your …
    > For …
    > And …
    > Do not let …
    > Bind …
    > Write …
    > So you will …
    > In the …
    > Trust …
    > And do not …
    > In all …
    > And He …
    > Do not be …
    > Fear …
    > It will be …
    > And …
    > Honor …
    > And from …
    > So your …
    > And your …
    > My son …
    > Or …

Week 7 Group Discussion

The following questions were posed after the lessons this past week. Take time to discuss the answers and ask for responses. Additional verses are listed which will give you, the teacher, more insight. These lists are not exhaustive. Feel free to pray and ask God for other verses that answer these questions for you. You can study these ahead of time and then either ask the students to look them up during class or just refer to them as you speak.

1. If someone chooses not to believe in the truth of the Bible does that make the Bible not true? (John 14:6). **Truth will always stand on its own. It is not subject to what someone thinks or feels about it. Four plus four equals eight every time whether you want to believe that or not. The truth of God, His Word, the life of Jesus, and eternity are set in stone. They cannot be altered by mere man's belief in them or not. What is *is*.**

2. Are there absolute truths? (Genesis 1:1, John 8:32). **According to the answer to number one, there are absolute truths. We must search these out and hold them up against God's word.**

3. Name some of these absolute truths. **God created us, God loves us, God provided a way to have a relationship with Him for eternity through the birth, life, death and resurrection of Jesus Christ, Satan is the Prince of the Power of the air, Satan will be defeated, morality does matter, etc.**

4. What are you doing now that you think God is using to equip you for some future work? (Jer. 29:11, Eph. 2:10, Phil. 1:6, 2 Tim. 2:21). **Answers will vary but may include teaching me to be patient, training me in a job skill, walking alongside me as I parent my children, trials and hardships that I might help others down the road (2 Cor. 1:3-4).**

5. Why does the foolish woman (and Satan) look to trap the righteous and not the foolish? (Matt. 12:30, Eph. 2:1-7, Col. 1:13). **The foolish already belong to Satan's camp. If he can trip up a Christian it ruins that Christian's ability to be effective for God's kingdom.**

6. Discuss the wise and foolish charts. **See appendices A and B.**

7. When you drive over the speed limit do you fear the policeman sitting on the corner?

8. When you sin, do you fear God? **As a Christian you do not have to fear the wrath of God (Rom. 8:1), but instead, your fear is to be a holy reverence for God (1 Peter 1:17-19). At the final judgment, all born again believers will be ushered into the kingdom of God.** Will you receive a crown? (1 Cor. 9:25, 1 Thess. 2:19-20, 2 Tim. 4:8, James 1:12, 1 Peter 5:1-4). **Crowns mentioned in the New Testament include The Crown of Incorruption for those who live a**

disciplined life; the Crown of Life for those who with patience endure trials; the Crown of Rejoicing for those who joyously expressed their faith; the Crown of Glory for those who are faithful in ministering the word of God; and the Crown of Righteousness for those who love Jesus' appearing (Rev. 2:10, 3:11).

9. Recite Proverbs 3:1-11.

Week 8

Week 8/Day 1 and Day 2: Comparison of Old and New Natures

OLD NATURE	NEW NATURE
condemned	salt of the earth
slave to sin	light of the world
immoral	children of God
impure	beloved of God
sensual	saints
idol worshiper	reign in life
sorcerer	freed from sin
one who practices enmity	not condemned
one who strives	heir of God
jealous	conquerors
angry	new creature
given to disputes	righteousness of God
dissentious	loving
causing faction	joyful
envious	peaceful
drunk	patient
carouser	kind
dead in trespasses and sins	good
son of disobedient	faithful
lived by lusts of flesh	gentle
indulged desires of flesh & mind	self-controlled
children of wrath	redeemed
futility of mind	forgiven
darkened in understanding	alive
excluded from God	raised up
ignorant	seated with Jesus in heaven
hard of heart	God's workmanship
callous	renewed in mind
greedy	likeness of God
bitter	righteous
wrathful	holy
clamorous	kind
given to slander	tender –hearted
malicious	forgiving
under wrath of God	strong in the Lord
wrathful	complete

malicious	dead to immorality
given to slander	dead to impurity
speaking abusively	dead to passions
liars	dead to evil desire
foolish	dead to greed
disobedient	renewed
deceived	chosen of God
enslaved	holy and beloved
hateful	washed clean
justified	
hopeful	
holy	
born again	
imperishable	
confident	

Questions to think about:

1. When you were born again, you put on a new nature. How often do you need to put this nature on? **Constantly**

2. Does freedom in Christ mean now you can do whatever you want to? Paul says that as sinners you were a slave to sin, but now you should be a slave to righteousness. **No. We are to be a living sacrifice to God through righteousness. Rom. 6:11-14.**

3. One more verse, and you will have memorized Proverbs 3:1-12. Add verse 12 to your Appendix C.

Week 8/Day 3: Freedom from Shame

According to Psalm 69:19, who knows about your shame? _____**God**_____

According to Psalm 71:1-3, where is this refuge? __**In God__ (See Ps. 91:1-4)**_____

Explain the following statement: "You are not a sinner because you sin, but you sin because you are a sinner." ____**Sin is the symptom of our sin nature. We have a sin nature, therefore, we sin. When we are born again, we can then choose not to sin through the power of Jesus.**_____

Would it have done any good to tell the old self to not lie, be peaceable, forgiving, etc.? Why or why not? __ **Maybe for a little while I could do better, but the disease of sin in the sin nature was still present and the symptoms of sinning would eventually come out.**_____

According to Philippians 3:13-14, what are we to forget? __**what lies behind**__

According to these verses what are you to reach forward to? __**what lies ahead**__

Questions to think about:

1. Does a Christian have any reason for shame from past or present actions? **No. Shame is connected to our sin which was dealt with at the cross.**

2. As a princess should you become haughty and selfish or serving and graceful? **A princess of the King of Kings should be serving and graceful in response to the gratitude she should feel for the sacrifice that was made for her by the blood of Jesus.**

3. Make a prayer box. Use any box such as a Kleenex box and decorate it. When you have a concern you need to turn over to God, write it on a piece of paper, pray about it, and put it in the box. If you start worrying about this matter or trying to figure it out, take the piece of paper out of the box, pray, and place the situation into God's hands again by putting the paper back into the box.

4. Recite your memorized verses and work on verse 12.

> My son …
> But let your …
> For …
> And …
> Do not let …
> Bind …
> Write …
> So you will …
> In the …
> Trust …
> And do not …
> In all …
> And He …
> Do not be …
> Fear …
> It will be …
> And …
> Honor …
> And from …
> So your …

And your …

My son …

Or …

For whom the Lord loves He ___**reproves**___,

Even as a father corrects the ___**son**___ in whom he ___**delights**___.

Week 8/Day 4: The Fear of the Lord

Do a quick review from the very beginning of this course. Fill in the blank from Proverbs 1:7. "The fear of the Lord is the beginning of ___**knowledge**___."

The fear of the Lord is the beginning of ___**wisdom**___; a good understanding has all those who do His commandments; His praise endures forever."

What do you think the fear of the Lord is based on according to these verses—His terrible anger and desire to see men pay for their sins? Or His righteousness, justice, and desire to see people repent and have a relationship with Him? ___**His righteousness, justice, and desire to see people repent and have a relationship with Him.**___

Psalm 112 will help you to answer the last question. From Psalm 112, list some of the things that will happen to the man that fears the Lord. (I found 18.)

Will be blessed	**never be shaken**
Descendants will be mighty	**be remembered forever**
Generation will be blessed	**not fear evil tidings**
Wealth	**will be steadfast**
Riches	**heart will be upheld**
Righteousness will endure	**no fear**
Light arises in darkness	**righteousness endures forever**
It is well	**horn will be exalted**
Maintain his cause in judgment	**will be honored**

It is the righteous in Christ that God refers to in Proverbs 15:29: "The Lord is far from the wicked, but He hears the ___**prayers**___ of the righteous."

Proverbs 15:8 states, "The ___**sacrifice**___ of the wicked is an ___**abomination**___ to the Lord, but the prayer of the upright is His delight."

In these verses what is the prerequisite for Jesus preparing you a place and coming back for you? ___**believe in God and in Jesus**___

Colossians 3:2 reiterates this principle. Write this verse here __**Set your mind on the things above, not on the things that are on earth.**__

Questions to think about:

1. What is the difference between knowing about Abraham Lincoln and knowing Abraham Lincoln? **Knowing about Lincoln is knowing the facts of his life. Only those who lived during his time and walked next to him could really know him.**

2. What is the difference between knowing about God and knowing God**? Knowing about God is having the facts. James 2:19 says that you do well to believe, "the demons also believe, and shudder." Knowing God is to have a personal relationship by entering into His presence through faith and praying and reading the Word of God.**

3. Pray for someone you know who knows about God, but needs to know Him personally.

4. Brush up on Proverbs 3:1-11 and keep working on 12.

> My son …
> But let your …
> For …
> And …
> Do not let …
> Bind …
> Write …
> So you will …
> In the …
> Trust …
> And do not …
> In all …
> And He …
> Do not be …
> Fear…
> It will be …
> And …
> Honor …
> And from …
> So your …
> And your …
> My son …

Or …

For whom the Lord ___loves_____ He __**reproves**_____ ,

Even as a __**father**___ corrects the __**son**___ in whom he ____**delights**_____ .

Week 8/Day 5: Now What?

Write out Colossians 3:23. _____**Whatever you do, do your work heartily, as for the Lord rather than for men.**_____

Look back at your verses in Colossians. In Colossians 3:16 what must richly dwell within you? ___**word of Christ**_____

How must the Word of God dwell within you? _____**richly**_____

Questions to think about:

1. What is one chore or task you have a hard time doing heartily as unto the Lord?

2. What praise song might you sing while doing this task that would make it more enjoyable?

3. Is God more interested in you getting your tasks done or your heart attitude as you do it? **Your heart's attitude**

4. Last day to perfect those memory verses.

> My son …
> But let your …
> For …
> And …
> Do not let …
> Bind …
> Write …
> So you will …
> In the …
> Trust …
> And do not…
> In all …
> And He …
> Do not be …
> Fear …

It will be …

And …

Honor …

And from …

So your …

And your …

My son …

Or …

For whom …

Even as …

Week 8 Group Discussion

The following questions were posed after the lessons this past week. Take time to discuss the answers and ask for responses. Additional verses are listed which will give you, the teacher, more insight. These lists are not exhaustive. Feel free to pray and ask God for other verses that answer these questions for you. You can study these ahead of time and then either ask the students to look them up during class or just refer to them as you speak.

1. When you were born again, you were given a new nature. How often do you need to put this nature on? **It is yours when you choose to accept Jesus as Lord and Savior – Rom. 10:9-10. Now you must practice using it–Col. 3:12-14).**

2. Does freedom in Christ mean now you can do whatever you want to? (Rom. 6:1- 2, 1 Corinthians 6:12, 10:23). **In regard to sin, our freedom is the ability to choose not to sin. In regard to other things that are not foundational such as type of music to worship by, color of carpet, whether or not to have a Christmas tree or celebrate Halloween, we have the freedom to choose. I might ask my child if they want a chocolate chip cookie or a raisin oatmeal cookie. Their choice will not affect our relationship and I will glory in their individuality and uniqueness.**

3. Does a Christian have any reason for shame from past actions? (Gen. 3:7, 10, Ps. 69:19, 2 Cor. 4:2, Phil.1:20, 1 John 2:28). **No, not if your sin has been confessed. Shame is directly related to sin. The sin was forgiven, so you no longer have to carry around your shame. It, too, must be laid at the foot of the cross. However, shame is one of Satan's weapons against you. He will tie you up with it and you will be unfruitful and unable to claim victory. You must realize that shame is a lie (once the sin has been dealt with) and replace that lie with God's truth of forgiveness, newness, being washed clean, and loved.**

4. Does a Christian have any reason for shame from present actions? (Eph. 4:1, 5:1-7, 1 John 1:9). **Conviction is from the Holy spirit and leads to repentance; condemnation is from Satan, shame is Satan's scam.**

5. How many times this week have you put a paper into your prayer box? (Week 8 Day 3).

6. What is the difference between knowing about God and knowing God? Ps. 46:10, James 2:19). **Only knowing God requires a relationship I can know about George Washington, but until I get to heaven and can sit with him and have tea, I will not know him. Knowing about God is having the facts, even believing them, but that is not enough. The demons know and believe in Jesus and yet, they shudder. To know God, I must sit with Him as I read His word and in prayer.**

7. Pray for someone you know who knows about God, but needs to know Him personally.

8. Recite Proverbs 3:1-12 aloud.

Foolishness: Characteristics and Results

	Characteristics	**Results**
1:7	despises wisdom and instruction	takes away life of its possessor
1:11	lies in wait for blood ambushes the innocent	
1:12	swallows them alive	
1:13	seeks for wealth and spoil	
1:16	feet run to evil Hasten to shed blood	
1:18		lie in wait for own blood ambush their own lives
1:19	gains by violence	violence takes away life of possessor
1:22	naïve simple minded scoffer hate knowledge	
1:29	hate knowledge did not choose the fear of the Lord	
1:30	not accept counsel spurns reproof	
1:32	wayward naïve complacent	will kill them be destroyed
2:16	strange flatters with words	

2:17	leaves companion of youth	
	forgets covenant of God	
2:18		house sinks to death
		tracks lead to the dead
2:19	do not return from sin	
	do not reach paths of life	
5:3	speech is smoother than oil; bitter - as wormwood	
5:4	sharp as two-edge sword	
5:5		death
5:6	unstable	
6:26	reduced to loaf of bread	loses precious life
6:27		be burned
6:28		be scorched
6:29	commits adultery	is punished
6:32	lacks sense	destroys himself
6:33		wounds and disgrace
		reproach not blotted out
		(people will remember his unfaithfulness)
6:34	jealous, enraged	
	takes vengeance	
6:35	does not accept ransom	
	not satisfied	
7:7	lacks sense	
7:8	takes way to house	
7:22	follows after sin	
7:23		loses life
3:7	wise is own eyes	
3:11	rejects Gods discipline	
	loathes His reproof	
3:32	crooked man	abomination
3:33	wicked	curse of God
3:34	scoffers	God scoffs at them
3:35	fools	dishonor
4:5	turns away from father's words	
4:16	do evil	can't sleep
		robbed of sleep

4:17	eat bread of wickedness	
	drink wine of violence	
4:24	deceitful mouth	
	devious speech	
5:9	gives vigor to others	
	gives years to the cruel one	
5:10		strangers filled with your - strength
		your handy work will go – to others' houses
5:11		will groan at end
5:12	hated instruction	
	heart spurned reproof	flesh and body will be consumed
5:13	not listened to teachings	
	did not listen to instructors	
5:14		utter ruin
5:22		will be captured
		will be held with chords of sin
5:23		die / will go astray
6:12	perverse mouth	
6:13	winking eye	
	signaling foot	
	pointing fingers	
6:14	devises evil	
	perverse heart	
	spreads strife	
6:15		calamity
		will be broken
		no healing
6:17	haughty eyes	
	lying tongue	
	hands that shed innocent blood	
6:18	heart that devises evil	
	feet run rapidly to evil	
6:19	false witness	
	liar	
	spreads strife among brothers	
6:25	desires beauty of adulteress – in heart	

6:26		reduced to a loaf of bread
6:27	life taking fire into bosom	clothes will be burned
6:28	like walking on hot coals	feet will be scorched
6:29	goes into neighbor's wife	will be punished
6:32	commits adultery	destroys himself
	lacks sense	
6:33		wounds
		disgrace
		reproach will not be –
		blotted out
6:34	jealous	
	enraged	
	does not spare his vengeance	
6:35	will not accept ransom	not satisfied
7:5	goes to adulteress	
7:7	lacks sense	
7:8	take way to sins house	
7:22	follows sin	
7:23		goes to be slaughtered
		cost his life
9:13	goes to boisterous sin	
9:17	drinks stolen water	
	eats bread in secret	
9:18		death

Appendix B

WISDOM: CHARACTERISTICS AND RESULTS

	<u>Characteristics</u>	<u>Results</u>
1:23	turns to reproof	God's Spirit
		know God's words
1:33	listens to God	lives securely
		be at ease from dread of evil
2:7	upright	sound wisdom
	walks in integrity	God will be shield
2:8	godly	
2:9	discerns righteousness	
	and justice and equity	
	and every good course	
2:10		wisdom will enter heart
		knowledge will be pleasant
2:11		guarded by discretion
		watched over by understanding
2:12		delivered from way of evil
		delivered from man who
		speaks perverse things
2:20	walks in way of good man	
	keeps to path of righteous	
2:21	upright	will live in land
	blameless	will remain in land
3:1	listens to father	
3:2	years of life	

		peace
		length of days
3:3	hangs on to kindness and truth	
3:4		favor, good repute
3:5	trusts God doesn't lean on own understanding	
3:6	acknowledge God	straight paths
3:7	fears God turns from evil	
3:8		healing to body
		Refreshment to bones
3:9	honors God with wealth	
3:10		barns filled
		vats overflowing
3:12		reproof
		God's love
3:13		finds wisdom
		gains understanding
3:16		long life
		riches / honor
3:17		pleasant ways
		peace
3:18		life / happiness
3:22		life
		adornment
3:23		walk securely
		will not stumble
3:24		not be afraid
		sweet sleep
3:25		no fear of fear
		no fear of wicked
3:26		confidence
		foot not caught
3:27	doesn't w/hold good	
3:29	doesn't devise harm against neighbor	
3:30	doesn't contend without cause	
3:32	upright	intimacy with God
3:33	righteous	house blessed

3:34	grace	
3:35	wise	honor
4:4	keeps commandments	life
4:5	acquires wisdom and understanding	
4:6	loves wisdom	guarded
4:8	prizes wisdom	exalted
	honors wisdom	be embraced
4:9	garland of grace	
	crown of beauty	
4:10	many years of life	
4:12	steps not impeded	
4:13	take hold of instruction	
	guards wisdom	
4:22		life
		health
4:25	eyes looking straight ahead	
4:26	watches the path of his feet	ways will be established
4:27	does not turn to right or left	
	turns foot from evil	
8:5		prudence
8:6		noble things
		right things
8:7		truthful
8:8		right
8:9		knowledge
		understanding
8:11		jewels
8:12		discretion
8:13		hates evil
		hates pride
8:14		sound counsel
		power
8:15		justice
8:17		love
8:18		riches
		honor
		wealth
8:21		generous

9:4		**turns to wisdom**
9:5	**eats and drinks wisdom**	
9:6	**forsakes folly**	**life, understanding**

Endnotes

1   *The American Heritage Dictionary of the English Language,* (retrieved from https://ahdictionary.com/word/search.html?q=wisdom, 2017).

2   *The American Heritage Dictionary of the English Language,* (retrieved from https://ahdictionary.com/word/search.html?q=prudent, 2017).

3   *Rules of Civility and Decent Behavior in Company and Conversation.* (Bedford, MA: Applewood Books, 1988).

4   Jan Silvious, *Foolproofing your Life,* (New York: Random House, Inc. 2009).

5   Laura I. Wilder, *Little House on the Prairie* (New York: HarperCollins, 1992).

6   Joni Erickson-Tada and Joe Musser, *Joni,* (Grand Rapids: Zondervan, 2001).

7   Corrie Ten Boom and Elizabeth and John Sherrill, *The Hiding Place,* (Grand Rapids: Chosen books, 1984).

8   Watchman Nee, *Sit, Walk, Stand,* (Fort Washington, PA: CLC Publications, 2009).

9   George Mueller, *The Autobiography of George Mueller,* (Kensington, Pa: Whitaker House, 1984).

10 Bruce Olsen, *Brushko,* (Powder Springs, GA: Creation House, 1993).

11 Brother Andrew and John Sherrill, *God's Smuggler,* (Bloomington, MN: Chosen Books, 2015).

12 Elisabeth Elliot, *Through Gates of Splendor,* (USA: Elisabeth Elliot, 1981).

13 James W. Sire, *The Universe Next Door,* (Downers Grove, IL: Intervarsity Press, 2009).

14 C.S. Lewis' *Mere Christianity,* (San Francisco: Harper, 2009).

15 Anabel Gillham, *The confident woman: Knowing Who You Are in Christ,* (Eugene, OR: Harvest House Publishers, 1993).

16 Jobe Martin, *Biblically Handling Technology and Social Media,* (Rockwall, TX: Biblical Discipleship Ministries, 2014).

17 William Thayer, *Gaining Favor with God and Man*, 1900 reprint. (Bulverde, TX: Mantle Ministries, no publ. date given), p. 57.

18 Melissa Dahl, NBC News Today, (retrieved from: http://www.today.com/health/many- marriedcouples-still-intensely-love-survey-finds-1C9381819).

19 Ruth Bell Graham, (retrieved from http://content.time.com/time/nation/article/0,8599,1633197,00.html).

20 William Harley, *His Needs/Her Needs*, 1986, (Grand Rapids: Revell, reprint 2011).

21 Emerson Eggerichs, *Cracking the Communication Code,* (Nashville: Thomas Nelson, 2007).

22 Emerson Eggerichs, *Love & Respect,* (Nashville: Thomas Nelson, 2004).

23 Gary Chapman, *The Five Love Languages,* 1992, (Chicago: Northfield Publishing, reprint 2015).

24 Walter Last, *The Neurochemistry of Sex,(* retrieved from http://www.health-science-spirit.com/neurosex.html).

25 Noah Webster, *Webster's 1913 Dictionary*, (retrieved from http://www.webster-dictionary.org/definition/surety).

26 Smithsonian website, (retrieved from https://www.si.edu/encyclopedia_si/nmnh/buginfo/bugnos.html).

27 Thayer, *Gaining Favor with God and Man*, p. 87.

28 Ibid. p. 57.

29 *The American Heritage Dictionary of the English Language,* (retrieved from https://ahdictionary.com/word/search.html?q=wperverse, 2017).

30 Francis Schaeffer, *The Mark of a Christian,* (Downers Grove, IL: Intervarsity Press, 1970).

31 Josh McDowell, *Evidence That Demands a Verdict,* (San Bernardino, CA: Here's Life Publishers, 1999).

32 *The American Heritage Dictionary of the English Language,* (retrieved from https://ahdictionary.com/word/search.html?q=boisterous, 2017).

If you want to continue your study of Proverbs, look for *Practical Proverbs for Women: Living Gracefully* which covers Proverbs 10-31 topically. Topics will include: nutrition, pride and humility, relationships, money, work ethic, welfare, budgeting, our words, anger management, forgiveness, marriage, raising children, the Proverbs 31 woman, and more.

About the Author

$\mathcal{D}$ara Halydier lives in Texas with her husband of 33 years. They have had many adventures together raising and homeschooling five boys, and they look forward to more escapades with their seven grandchildren. Dara has been a pastor's wife, mentor, leader of homeschool groups, piano teacher, and friend. She has learned spiritual lessons the hard way—experience! She battles chronic pain with spina bifida and numerous back surgeries, survived and thrives after a childhood of abuse, and loves to sing the praises of her Father God.

Made in the USA
Columbia, SC
28 February 2018